TRANSACTIONS

OF THE

AMERICAN PHILOSOPHICAL SOCIETY

HELD AT PHILADELPHIA
FOR PROMOTING USEFUL KNOWLEDGE

NEW SERIES—VOLUME 66, PART 8
1976

CROWN AND COMMONWEALTH

A STUDY IN THE OFFICIAL ELIZABETHAN DOCTRINE
OF THE PRINCE

EDWARD O SMITH, JR.
Associate Professor of History, State University College at Buffalo

THE AMERICAN PHILOSOPHICAL SOCIETY
INDEPENDENCE SQUARE
PHILADELPHIA

November, 1976

To
EDWARD JOHN DREA

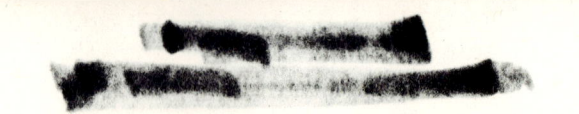

Copyright © 1976 by The American Philosophical Society
Library of Congress Catalog
Card Number 76-24258
International Standard Book Number 0-87169-668-1
US ISSN 0065-9746

ACKNOWLEDGMENTS

Research for this book was made possible by a grant-in-aid from the Research Foundation of the State University of New York. The editors of the *Anglican Theological Review, The Historical Magazine of the Protestant Episcopal Church,* and the *Huntington Library Quarterly* have graciously granted permission to use work previously published in their respective journals.

The staffs of the Folger Shakespeare Library; the Public Record Office; Lambeth Palace Library; the Library Company of Philadelphia; Lehigh University Library; Widener Library; the Law Library, Eighth Judicial District, Buffalo, New York; and the Edward H. Butler Library, Buffalo State College, were most helpful in facilitating work on this study. Special appreciation is due to colleagues who offered their invaluable knowledge and talent: Marjorie Gesner, Melvin Tucker, George Keiser, Robert Lorenz, John Aiken, Edmund A. Brown, and Michael Riccards. To Patricia Warner and Carol Julian, I am indebted for their careful work in preparing and typing the manuscript.

E.O.S., Jr.

CROWN AND COMMONWEALTH: A STUDY IN THE OFFICIAL ELIZABETHAN DOCTRINE OF THE PRINCE

Edward O. Smith, Jr.

CONTENTS

Introduction: The Royal Mystique	5
I. The Lord's Anointed	10
II. Defender of the Faith	17
III. Prince, Parliament, and People	30
IV. Our Dread Sovereign Lady	43
Index	51

INTRODUCTION

THE ROYAL MYSTIQUE

The Wilton Diptych in the National Gallery in London is a fine expression of the essence of later medieval kingship. On the left obverse panel is King Richard II, youthful and handsome, clothed in a gown ornamented with his white hart and other devices, kneeling on the the ground, his hands raised and slightly open. Behind him stand St. John the Baptist with his hand on the king's shoulder, and St. Edward the Confessor. To the left of the Confessor is another royal saint, St. Edmund of East Anglia. This group of four is placed in a deserted landscape with a clump of dark trees visible behind the Baptist. The right-hand panel of the obverse side shows the Virgin and Child with eleven angels walking on a lawn covered with flowers. They appear to be advancing on the figures in the opposite panel. Three angels point towards the king while another holds a banner with the red cross on a white ground. Each of the angels is wearing the white hart badge, emblem of Richard II. The Christ Child appears to beckon the king with a blessing.[1]

Painted after 1400 in the international Gothic style, the Diptych is a splendid blend of heraldic and naturalistic elements which permit a closer iconographic analysis. First, the special relationship of the king to his patron saint John the Baptist is marked. Second, the monarch's special devotion to St. Edward the Confessor is indicated. Third, the Confessor himself is presented as "the grand old king," the patriarch of the royal house of Richard II. Fourth, St. Edmund, martyred by the unbelieving Danes, is present as a reminder of the duty of kings to the true faith. Fifth, the presence of the two royal Saxon saints emphasizes the special interest which English monarchs, including Richard II, took in their ancient and noble lineage.

Taken together, the four figures suggest that Richard II is being presented to the Virgin by his patron saint and by his saintly ancestors.

This presentation is complemented by the right panel in which the Virgin and Child are welcoming the king. The eleven angels, wearing their hart badges, are his appointed companions. The purpose of this memorial picture—to show the transference of Richard II from his earthly kingdom to his heavenly kingdom—is further confirmed as the dark woods which are behind the Baptist in the left panel are seen as a signification of the earthly life. Moreover, the transference of the king to the second panel would increase to twelve the number of figures which surrounded the Virgin and Child and underscore the fact that the angelic company are intended as companions to Richard. Carrying the banner of redemption, these angels await their new member and companion. Finally, the analysis is supported by the youthful idealized portrait of the king himself. For this representation emphasizes that the beholder is witnessing a scene not of this world. Richard has received his portion with those saints who have been pleasing to the King of Kings; he who was crowned in this world receives a crown in the next; he who was blessed here is now blessed there.

The importance of the Wilton Diptych to the present study is that it visually expresses the essence of regality as held by many in fifteenth-century Catholic England and by many in sixteenth-century Protestant England. Whether official or unofficial in its inspiration, the picture clearly stresses the exaltation of the monarch. And this exaltation is multidimensional: it is temporal and eternal, terrestrial and celestial, individual and archetyphal. Not only a manifestation of deeply held truths, the picture is also a contribution to the elucidation and perpetuation of those truths which are necessary for a proper understanding of the nature of regality. Its most crucial contribution, therefore, is its way of apprehending and comprehending reality. Clearly its focus is on Richard II, but to achieve this focus, it draws upon the relevant intellectual and psychological elements of a great model of reality. The themes this artist of the last Plantagenet develops are akin to those treated by a dramatist of the last Tudor's reign when he wrote:

Not all the water in the rough rude sea
Can wash the balm off from an anointed king;
The breath of worldly men cannot depose
The deputy elected by the Lord.

(Rich.II:III:II:54–57)

---

[1] Francis Wormald, "The Wilton Diptych," *Jour. Warburg and Courtauld Institutes* 17 (1954): pp. 191–203. The analysis of the diptych is based on this article.

Both men were nourished from the riches of this model; both drew upon it to illumine facets of the image of regality; and both contributed to the viability of the English royal mystique.

The veneration, exaltation, and even deification of kings and emperors, Kantorowicz and Geanakoplos have suggested, were common to both the Latin west and Byzantine east.[2] Fitting into this broad medieval Christian pattern, England likewise had her special sacred kings and her recurring cults of kingship as the Wilton Diptych illustrates. The mystique which emerges around the nature and person of the monarch was often spontaneous and popular in origin, yet periodically reflected official cultivation and inspiration. In the sixteenth century, probably the most sustained and successful of these official English efforts was that of the Elizabethan era. Scholars have commented frequently upon the tremendous adulation and veneration directed towards the Virgin Queen by her various subjects in and out of positions of official responsibility. Indeed, the popular element in the cult of the Virgin Queen cannot be denied, and its existence allowed officials to cultivate this seedbed of monarchical exaltation for their own purposes.[3]

The official concept of kingship which emerged under Elizabeth then was a cluster of ideas, attitudes, and values which formed a normative intellectual system plus a set of non-rational actions and behavior patterns which, when taken together, formed the royal mystique. For sustenance, it drew upon the medieval model of the universe as this was accepted and simplified in the sixteenth century. Despite the ideological issues raised by the Reformation, this model remained a frame in which the polemics of Catholics and Protestants could be intelligently and heatedly conducted. The very didactic quality of the model, its informative and instructional thrust, provided riches for those seeking to divine rightly the proper ways of equipping men to be good and useful citizens of the earthly city and the heavenly city. Thus More could criticize the sterility of the scholastics, Hooker could find succor in Aquinas, and all could denounce Machiavelli. The medieval and Elizabethan model, therefore, provided many concepts for communal and self-understanding, but the most vital of these appeared as a great chain of being, a set of correspondences, and a cosmic dance. To these highly theoretical and practical concepts were added those of sin and redemption to complete the idea clusters which comprehended all aspects of reality or being. The subsidiary concepts of order, degree, and hierarchy and their converse ideas of rebellion, anarchy, and chaos also supported the mystique.[4]

Like the spacious medieval model upon which it rested, the official Elizabethan royal mystique was syncretistic and synthetic in character. Seeking neither logical nor purely rational consistency, it achieved psychological and sociological integration. Past patterns were blended with more recent contributions which reflected altered social and political circumstances. Ideological and intellectual expressions inimical to the well-being of the commonwealth as officially conceived were rejected. Thus this official Elizabethan concept of kingship was a powerful set of conservative ideas and values which were both normative and coercive in nature. Its major aspects—sacred and secular— were derivative of the traditional *sacerdotium* and *regnum* and defined the relationships between ruler and ruled in their external corporate nature and in their internal individual nature to effect a state in which society could flourish devoid of extremism. In this sense, the official Elizabethan mystique was in its intellectual significance not unlike the *via media* was in its institutional significance. It illustrated the point made by Dickens in *The English Reformation* that church and state were "always fighting the moral and social battle side by side," however much each fought with the other.[5] In this battle, monarchs played a central role, one clearly discernible in the mystique, for the queen was its matrix, uniting the sacred and profane natures in her person.

The development of the sacred aspect of kingship was preeminently the work of the Church. Orthodox, Catholic, and Protestant theologians and liturgists provided numerous interpretations and analyses of the divinity which surrounded rulers, and thereby emphasized the theocratic nature of society. Geanakoplos in *Byzantine East and Latin West: Two Worlds of Christendom in Middle Ages and Renaissance* has noted the ramifications of this problem in eastern theology.

---

[2] Ernst H. Kantorowicz, *The King's Two Bodies A Study in Mediaeval Political Theology* (Princeton, 1957); and Deno J. Geanakoplos, *Byzantine East and Latin West: Two Worlds of Christendom in Middle Ages and Renaissance* (Oxford, 1966), especially chap. 2.

[3] J. E. Neale, *Essays in Elizabethan History* (New York, 1958), pp. 9–20, 45–58; Roy C. Strong, "The Popular Celebration of the Accession Day of Queen Elizabeth I," *Jour. Warburg and Courtauld Institutes* 21 (1958): pp. 86–103; and Francis Yates, "Elizabethan Chivalry: The Romance of the Accession Day Tilts," *Jour. Warburg and Courtauld Institutes* 20 (1957): pp. 4–25.

[4] The intellectual assumptions of the age are discussed in C. S. Lewis, *The Discarded Image: An Introduction to Medieval and Renaissance Literature* (Cambridge, 1964); E. M. W. Tillyard, *The Elizabethan World Picture* (New York, 1944); Theodore Spencer, *Shakespeare and the Nature of Man* (New York, 1942); and in James Winney, ed., *The Frame of Order* (London, 1957). Douglas Bush, *The Renaissance and English Humanism* (Toronto, 1939), and C. S. Lewis, *English Literature in the Sixteenth Century Excluding Drama* (Oxford, 1954), offer considerable insight into the intellectual problems of the period. Rosamond Tuve, *Allegorical Imagery: Some Medieval Books and Their Posterity* (Princeton, 1966), points up problems of method and definition on pp. 3–55, especially pp. 21–33; which are relevant to this study.

[5] A. G. Dickens, *The English Reformation* (London, 1964), p.14.

The work clearly showed the distinctive governing and administrative functions of the emperor and stressed his unique position among laymen symbolized in his liturgical privileges. Through the coronation, the emperor attained a kind of "hieratic character" but did not make him a cleric. In relation to what the author describes as the "esoteric form of the Church," that is, its dogmatic and sacramental integrity, the emperor had no authority. His relation to the Church, therefore, was analogous to that of the medieval English monarch. The emperor, the author noted, occupied a position in the *sacerdotium* and *regnum* akin to that conveyed in the title of Elizabeth I: Queen by the Grace of God, Defender of the Faith, and Supreme Governor of the Church.

Ernst Kantorowicz in his *The King's Two Bodies: A Study in Medieval Political Theology,* has also suggested a similar set of functions for princes in western theological thought. The monarch assumed frequently the attributes of Christ as a mediator and link between his people and God, between the temporal and eternal orders. To the extent that these concepts rested upon sacramental and liturgical thought, the ruler took on a unique sacramental quality evidenced in the coronation or consecration orders and manifested in the *laudes regiae* sung to his renown.[6] The king was hypostatized in the king who never dies, an idea clearly seen in the Wilton Diptych and in Shakespeare's lines previously cited. The thrust of western liturgical and theological expression, therefore, was to create a king who had two natures analogous to those of Christ, one human, the other divine.

As emphasis on the consecrational transformation of the king increased, a clericalization of the king and his office occurred. J. Wickham Legg specifically indicated this fact in reference to English sovereigns and suggested that it also reflected the official French view as late as 1775. The king was a *persona mixta* in England and "la première personne Ecclésiastique de son Royaume" in France.[7] Guerard likewise made a similar point about the sixteenth-century strength of French monarchical theory. One major component which assisted the ruler was the idea that he was the Lord's anointed, like David and the royal line of Israel. The heavenly origin of regal power had its earthly signs, the author noted: "the holy chrism used at his coronation imparted to him a sacred character. His touch cured 'the King's evil.'"[8]

The concepts of king as *persona mixta* and as mediator continued to be important to the theological and liturgical contributions of the Elizabethan Church to the royal mystique. Those liturgical efforts which surrounded Elizabeth continued the virility of medieval religious art and drama, the power of which, Dickens observed, lay in the pictorial presentation of Christian belief.[9] For example, the Catholic coronation of the *Liber Regalis* and the Protestant orders of the *Book of Common Prayer,* together with occasional services officially prescribed, exhibited a fundamental unity of concept about regality. Furthermore, the medieval *laudes regiae* had their Elizabethan equivalents in the occasional services, especially those of the Accession Day. Although worship services of the Established Church might emphasize the Protestant notion of the "godly prince," they did not supplant the inherited liturgical forms or modes of thought. The new emphasis was a more striking statement of previously received typologies, for whether seen from a Catholic or a Protestant liturgical stance, Elizabeth still remained the anointed of the Lord and mediator between God and the people.

The occasional services of the Church of England made a distinctive contribution to the liturgical tradition as they were so frequently associated with great moments of national tragedy and triumph. The most notable of these services was that devised to celebrate the Accession Day of Elizabeth. While the Anglican Church denigrated the veneration of the saints and the cult of the Virgin Mary, it accommodated itself through such services to the needs of folk religious sentiment previously fulfilled by the medieval cults. As the *Liber Regalis* and the *Prayer Book* stressed the stern masculinity of regality, so the Accession Day services showed the gracious femininity of sovereignty. The needs fulfilled by the cult of the Virgin Mary were now satisfied liturgically by the cult of the Virgin Elizabeth. (The monarch as mediator was also the monarch as mediatrix.) The criticisms of extremists, Catholic and Puritan, of the Accession Day celebrations emphasized unwittingly the success of the Established Church in bridging the cultural and chronological gap between Catholic and Protestant pieties. As Strong has shown, Catholic criticism held that the celebrations derogated from devotion due the Virgin Mary, while Puritan censure decried the deification of Elizabeth which detracted from the worship of Christ. Both criticisms show the psychological significance of the Accession Day celebrations, for the needs of popular religion and official policy were synthesized. The Queen's Day replaced the Lady Day; the office of the Virgin Mary had its substitute in the office of the Virgin Queen;

---

[6] For a discussion of the liturgical side of western medieval kingship, see Ernst H. Kantorowicz, *Laudes Regiae: A Study in Liturgical Acclamations and Mediaeval Ruler Worship* (Berkeley and Los Angeles, 1958).

[7] J. Wickham Legg, "The Sacring of the English Kings," *Archaeol. Jour.* (1894): p. 28 and n. 4.

[8] Albert Guerard, *France in the Classical Age* (New York, 1965), p. 64.

[9] Dickens, *English Reformation,* p. 11. Chapter 1 provides an illuminating discussion of late medieval piety and the emphases of the Protestant reformers pertinent to some of the following observations.

Marian hymns gave place to metrical thanksgivings; the *Stella Maris* became the *Stella Britannis*.[10]

The theological dimension supplied the doctrine of the godly prince to the mystique. Although this doctrine was not unknown to medieval thought, the Anglican formulation emerged consonant with the modes of thought and expression derived from the Reformation legacy. The position of the prince in the esoteric form of the Church was minimized or overlooked. Instead, stress was placed on the role of the king in the external form of the Church. The relationship of ruler and ruled was established and the public and private responsibilities of each defined. A balance was sought between the polemics of Catholics and the strictures of Puritans, a stance which found ultimate expression in Hooker. Although allegorical, typological, and historical elements were present, the theological exposition tended to be highly scriptural, especially Pauline, in quality. Humanistic exegesis and Protestant modalities were united.

Although didactic, devotional, and polemical works often elaborated the official doctrine of the godly prince, the most frequent and effective means of exposition was homiletical. The *Book of Homilies* and the sermons of the episcopate represent the clearest and most authoritative formulation of the doctrine and link this concept most directly and intimately to the liturgical concepts. Thus, in its liturgical and theological efforts, the Church presented a perspective on the nature of regality which drew upon the rich legacy of medieval imagery and pictorial presentation. To these, it added the tools of humanist scholarship, the preoccupations of Protestant theology, and the most advanced methods of communication to aid in the articulation and dissemination of its teachings about the sacredness of kingship.

The political and legal components which made up the profane side of the royal mystique did not escape the normative influence of theology and liturgy. Kantorowicz has shown this point in medieval political and legal thought and has noted the concepts of the *regnum* paralleled those of the *sacerdotium*. The king became hypostatized with his policy or with his law. Even the early Tudor theory of kingship which Baumer analyzed showed the vitality, continuity, and utility of the ideas and values presented by Kantorowicz, in meeting novel circumstances poised by the breach with Rome. By the reign of Elizabeth, these older and newer ideas were synthesized and sustained by received ecclesiological models common to the broader European tradition.[11]

The often mystical expressions of the ecclesiological patterns served Tudor and Elizabethan statesmen and lawyers well. Dunham has pointed out how these men often treated the mystical marriage of prince and people through the concept of the crown imperial.[12] Hence, Thomas Smith could treat the commonwealth as a body with the queen as head and the subjects as members united together for a common purpose. The whole series of formal and informal relationships between these parts of the commonwealth could be subsumed under a constitutional concept of the Queen in Parliament. Likewise, Burghley in his *Execution of Justice* could try to defend the government's religious policy and try to refute erroneous ideological interpretations of the nature of the commonwealth. Even Thomas Wilson in his work on usury sought to emphasize the moral obligations and responsibilities operative between prince and people. Yet, the finest blend of normative and pragmatic elements in the political sphere lay in royal speeches.

The theoretical expositions, the calculated apologetics, and the patriotic moralisms of the statesmen together with the ethical pragmatism of royal utterances illustrated a desire to reconcile eternal verities with current exigencies. Naturally, surface appearances did not always provide logical consistency. What gave life to such concepts as the commonwealth, the crown imperial, the royal supremacy, or the royal dignity and estate was the prince. While the dynamics of social change might influence the utterances of sovereign and statesmen and while the demands of policy might shape their words, still behind these considerations they saw the commonwealth as a sublime metaphor. It was like the Mystical Body of Christ and His Church; it was the union of husband and wife. Ultimately, this prince and people would be seen as a corporation sole.

The importance of the political component of the mystique has been well set out by Dunham in "The Crown Imperial" and by Kantorowicz in "Mysteries of State."[13] Both have shown the English and continental efforts to match inherited ideas with immediate needs. These ethical and utilitarian concerns of statecraft were integral to the thought of Elizabeth and her advisers. Moreover, both authors have indicated that such concerns frequently sought legal expression. For, while theologians and liturgists supplied the soul, and princes and statesmen the flesh and blood, judges and jurists provided the bone and sinew of regality.

---

[10] Strong, "Popular Celebration," *Jour. Warburg and Courtauld Institutes* 21: pp. 95-101. For the relation of the Virgin Mary to the Virgin Queen in literature, see also Thomas P. Roche, Jr., *The Kindly Flame: A Study of the Third and Fourth Books of Spenser's Faerie Queene* (Princeton, 1964), pp. 141-142.

[11] See Kantorowicz, *The King's Two Bodies*, mentioned above, as well as Franklin Le Van Baumer, *The Early Tudor Theory of Kingship* (New Haven, 1940). See also J. W. Allen, *A History of Political Thought in the Sixteenth Century* (London, 1928); and Christopher Morris, *Political Thought in England, Tyndale to Hooker* (London, 1957).

[12] William Huse Dunham, Jr., "'The Crown Imperial,'" *Parliamentary Affairs* 6: pp. 199-206.

[13] Ernst H. Kantorowicz, "Mysteries of State An Absolutist Concept and Its Late Mediaeval Origins," *Harvard Theol. Rev.* 48 (1955): pp. 65-91; and Dunham, "The Crown Imperial," cited above.

The juridical understanding of kingship was forthrightly stated in the decision of the judges in the Duchy of Lancaster case in 1562. The importance of this decision, Holdsworth observed, was its elaboration of the distinction between the politic and natural functions of the king. As the opinion expressed it,

the king has in him two bodies, viz. a body natural, and a body politic. His body natural (if it be considered in itself) is a body mortal, subject to all infirmities that come by nature or accident, to imbecility of infancy or old age, and to the like defects that happen to the natural bodies of other people. But his body politic is a body that cannot be seen or handled, consisting of policy and government, and constituted for the direction of the people, and the management of the public weal; and this body is utterly void of infancy and old age, and other natural defects and imbecilities, which the body natural is subject to, and for this cause, what the king does in his body politic cannot be invalidated or frustrated by any disability in his natural body.[14]

The judges also stated that the king's natural body was invested with the estate and dignity royal. It was magnified when it was conjoined with his body politic which contained the office, government, and majesty royal. The king, therefore, was a kind of *corporation sole* but not necessarily equated with or identified with the modern concept of the state. Maitland might deride this concept as "metaphysiological nonsense," but the idea conveyed a way of looking at the nature of kingship which was not incongruous with ecclesiastical expressions.[15] Furthermore, this legal fiction illustrated the dominance of inherited modalities of thought and provided an English cognate of those continental models based on Roman law, which strove to enlarge the concept of the prince commensurate with societal demands.

The exalted doctrine of the prince so crucial to the property law in the Duchy of Lancaster case was also the center of the criminal law. From the princely center, the criminal law drew a circle of definitions which established what acts were in conformity with the duties owed by the individual to the community. The highest expression of such duties was in the relationship between ruler and subject. Within the criminal law the most salient Elizabethan statement of these theoretical and practical relationships was the law of treason. To the extent that this law rested upon the great treasons statute of Edward III, it demonstrated continuity of concept when applied in the case law or a point of departure when developed through the enacted law. Together, therefore, common and statutory elements reflected the hallowed tradition to preserve the nation personified in the prince under the altered circumstances of Reformation England. Moreover, the concepts of the treason law reflected an official response to what Dunham has cogently posed as the paradox of regalian power and the rule of law.[16] The liberty of the subject and the preservation of the sovereign required resolution in these legal concepts. The ever well-intended prince confronted the oft-times malevolent liege man; justice with mercy and truth with equity demanded synthesis. The conceptual resolution of these paradoxes was the juridical contribution to the official mystique.

In the law of treason, the normative and utilitarian values of the official concept of kingship were united with the coercive ones. Confrontation between queen and recalcitrant subject was initiated, processed, and resolved according to the substance and procedure of the law. Like a liturgical drama, the legal one bore witness to the general acceptance of the official views on regality. As Lacey Smith has shown, the ritual-like confessions of the convicted, with their acts of contrition and pleas for reconciliation with the sovereign evidenced the deep penetration of normative values. For even the most alienated, the most unsocialized members of the commonwealth had in some measure themselves internalized the values offered them. In death, these tormented individuals achieved at last complete socialization with the looked-for salvation of their souls.[17]

The sacred and profane components of the official Elizabethan concept of the prince, with their underlying modalities of thought, were an expression then of what Sorokin has designated as the Idealistic mentality and culture. In such a mentality and culture, the underlying system of truth is a mix between supersensory revelation and sensory evidence, that is, the truth of faith is synthesized with the truth of the senses. Both

---

[14] Sir William Holdsworth, *A History of English Law* (London, 1966) 4: pp. 202–203.

[15] Frederic William Maitland, *The Collected Papers,* ed. H. A. L. Fisher (Cambridge, 1911), 3: p. 249 in the essay "The Crown as Corporation." The concept *dignitas* had a long history in which the dignity of the king emerged from that of an ecclesiastical person, especially an abbot. The idea implied the dual nature of the person, one immortal, the other mortal. To the extent that property was involved, it was assumed to be held under the immortal nature of the person. In English law, the estate and dignity royal derived from this juridical-theological view. Hence, lands or corporeal things were subject to the immortal rights of the king as expressed in the concept of his "body politic." Moreover, the English kings in the natural bodies were united with the king in his body politic so that king and crown tended to become equivalent ideas. Thus, the king never dies; rather, there is a demise of the crown in which the local temporal body of a natural king is separated from the immortal, incorporeal body politic and reunited to a new natural body of another natural king. Thus, the incorporeal hereditaments of the king are never impaired by the nonage or old age, for example, of a given natural body like Elizabeth I.

[16] William Huse Dunham, Jr., "Regal Power and the Rule of Law," *Jour. British Studies* 3 (1964): pp. 24–56 presents a brilliant analysis of the role of statesmen and jurists who had formulated "the medieval principle of lawful procedure into that of due process; and . . . had transmuted that vague concept, the supremacy of law, into 'The certain rule of law'" (p. 56).

[17] Lacey B. Smith, "English Treason Trials and Confessions in the Sixteenth Century," *Jour. Hist. of Ideas* 15 (1954): pp. 471–498.

sources of truth are united and reconciled according to the "logical laws of the human mind which itself, in a sense, has a vein of divine nature." Revelation, reason, and senses form this mixed model so that all references to these three sources of truth "tend to show that their testimony is unanimous and that they do not contradict one another."[18] Its method of exposition is primarily dialectic and deductive. Certainly, the Elizabethan concept of kingship illustrates these points as well as showing evidence of apodictic and symbolic characteristics associated with the ideational truth of faith. Little in the official formulations rested on induction and experimentation so essential, Sorokin argued, to the sensate system of truth. Little in its modalities separated it from the broader European ones associated with the mixed Idealistic model.

The official concept had relevance in terms of mass organizational typologies.[19] The ecclesiastical structure emerged as a normative one which sought to pervade all Elizabethan society with its salutary values. The political structure, seen as the Queen in Parliament, likewise tried to penetrate society with a set of utilitarian objectives that engaged individual commitment for the success of the commonwealth, its proper functioning, and its survival. Ultimately, the coercive typology, embodied in the legal system, was prevaded by the values and goals of the first two types. Its object was to cope with deviant behavior or alienation which resulted from the imperfect efforts of normative and utilitarian organizational expressions to complete socialization. In the concept of the prince, these three typologies were united and had a common center for their respective uses of power. Ambiguities and uncertainties thrust upon the commonwealth from many sources could ultimately find intellectual and emotional resolution in the official concept of kingship. Specific and ambiguous in nature, the official doctrine provided a set of ideas and values which engaged not only the great mass but also the reactionary and radical fringes of Elizabethan society, for all shared the same Idealistic mentality, and all were confronted by the same center, Elizabeth I.

In the discussion of the official concept of kingship which follows, certain limitations have been set on the types of material included. First, works of doubtful authorship have been excluded. Second, books and tracts of a highly polemical and theological nature have been omitted. These limitations are designed to avoid sensational, dubious, and exaggerated expressions in favor of more familiar, routine, and normal statements of the official doctrine. Given these restrictions, the material examined in this study falls into two major divisions: that which is temporal in nature and that which is ecclesiastical.

The spiritual order developed the concept of kingship through its normal liturgical and homiletical functions. Therefore, the study includes, first, an analysis of the public and private forms of worship established by authority during the reign of Elizabeth. Second, since the sermon literature is very extensive, the study deals only with sermons preached by men who held sees under Elizabeth and sermons or homilies appointed by authority.

Since the number of temporal officers was large, it is possible to consider only the works of those who held high political posts in the Elizabethan government. To this discussion has been added a consideration of the queen's speeches before Parliament. Finally, the contribution of the Parliament and the judges to the official concept of kingship is examined as this was elaborated in the law of treason, the most representative formulation of the obligations of prince and people so integral to the official theory.

I. THE LORD'S ANOINTED

The coronation festivities of Elizabeth I provided the first formal, elaborate, and enthusiastic expression of the official view of kingship of the reign. These ceremonies were important because they emphasized both the sacred and secular elements of the royal doctrine. The rich intellectual legacy of the past was employed in the service of the present through a series of ceremonies which captured the imagination of the people, quickened the sense of national unity, and inspired awe and reverence for the prince. The secular aspect was well illustrated by the royal procession from the Tower to Westminster on the day before the coronation. On this occasion, ample opportunity existed for the ruler to show herself to the applauding crowds and for them to respond with suitable pageants and tableaux which exhibited their hopes and aspirations for the new reign. The themes developed on that day were ones which could be and were developed in greater detail throughout the queen's long reign. Thus, this procession gave a glimpse of, and was a prelude to a much fuller elaboration of, the official concept of the prince.

The coronation itself reflected the legacy of the past and bore witness to the sense of tradition and continuity so much a part of the Elizabethan world view. The product of Catholic piety about kingship, the service of consecration was now used for a Protestant queen. Its very use emphasized the fact that ultimately the nature of regality transcended narrow ideological and partisan controversy which was inevitably associated with the Reformation era. Moreover, the service was a splendid liturgical drama which acted out the great theological, legal, and theoretical truths about the na-

---

[18] Pitrim A. Sorokim, *Social and Cultural Dynamics* (New York, 1937) **2**: p. 6. See his discussion in chap. 1.

[19] Amitai Etzioni in his *A Comparative Analysis of Complex Organizations*, (Glencoe, Ill., 1961), provides a most helpful set of typologies for understanding the relationship of power and structures. These models alluded to in the text have considerable pertinence in understanding Elizabethan theory and its institutional expressions.

ture of monarchy, which rested upon common intellectual assumptions. Thus, the coronation service was a most exquisite dance, reminiscent of the great cosmic one that showed the very nature of reality in action.

Taken together, the procession to Westminster and the coronation service itself provided an opportunity for the elaboration of the official position of kingship and provided a series of themes which formed the nucleus of ideas systematically presented throughout the reign. It is the purpose of this chapter, therefore, to examine the major ideas presented in the pageants associated with the royal procession and then to consider those enunciated in the coronation service as this was contained in the *Liber Regalis,* a compendium of liturgical services pertaining to the monarchy.[1]

1.

On Saturday, January 14, 1559, the royal procession moved from the tower to Westminster. The City of London was like "a Stage wherein was shewed the wonderful Spectacle of a noble hearted Princess towards her most loving people; and the people's exceeding comfort in beholding so worthy a Sovereign."[2] The first pageant awaited Elizabeth at Gracechurch, its theme was unity and concord. A three-tiered stage depicted Henry VII and Elizabeth of York on the lowest tier; the middle one portrayed Henry VIII and Anne Boleyn; and Elizabeth appeared on the highest level. Out of the unity of the two roses of Lancaster and York emerged the delicate bloom Elizabeth, symbol of unity and concord. A child revealed the message to the queen and other onlookers, pointing out that as the union of these great houses had ended civil war and bloodshed, so now the queen's subjects trusted she would stint present discontent and increase quietness.

"The Seat of Worthy Government" was the subject of the second presentation at Cornhill. Here a child appearing as the queen was placed on a seat of government supported by four persons. Each figure represented a virtue which trampled its contrary vice under foot. Pure religion, love of subjects, wisdom, and justice overcame the vices of ignorance and superstition, rebellion and insolence, folly and vainglory, adulation and bribery, respectively. The message was most clear: Elizabeth's people hoped that these virtues would maintain her throne "that good with good may joy, and naught with naught may moan!" The suppression of vice and evil and the exaltation of true religion and godly virtue were essential for the security of prince and people, the stability of the seat of government, and the health of the nation. The first two pageants, therefore, rested heavily upon the experience of history and the lessons of mortality while the next one had a different focus.[3]

As Elizabeth reached the Great Conduit in Cheap, she saw "The Eight Beatitudes, Expressed in the Fifth Chapter of the Gospel of Saint Matthew, Applied to Our Sovereign Lady Queen Elizabeth." Here children on a three-tiered stage drew the appropriate lessons. The queen's past conduct had indicated that these blessings might befall her. If she continued in this pattern now, she most certainly would receive the Gospel blessings:

Thou has been eight times blest! O Queen of worthy fame!
By Meekness in thy spirit, when care did thee beset!
By Mourning in thy grief! by Mildness in thy blame!
By Hunger and by Thirst, and justice couldst none get!
By Mercy showed, not felt! by cleanness of thy heart!
By seeking Peace always! by Persecution wrong!
Therefore, trust thou in God! since He hath helped thy smart!
That, as His Promise is, so He will make thee strong![4]

To moral virtue was now added the promise of spiritual grace for the ruler and for the people, truly a glorious prospect.

The societal implications of the preceding pageants were highlighted in the one presented at the Little Conduit in Cheap. Time was its center, commonwealths its concern, two hills its setting. One of these hills was cragged, barren, stony, and contained a withered and dead tree. A mournful, rudely dressed youth, named "Ruinosa Respublica, A Decayed Common Weal," sat under the withered tree. The second hill, verdant, fair, and flourishing, contained a fruitful tree under which stood a well-appareled handsome youth named "Respublica Bene Instituta, A Flourishing Common Weal." Between these hills was a cave from which Father Time and the Daughter of Time emerged. Out of the rock Father Time brought his daughter who held a book, "The Word of Truth." At last, the moral suggested, Time had once again brought forth the Truth that all hoped Elizabeth would embrace. Moreover, all hoped she would see the lessons

---

[1] The coronation has received considerable attention among scholars. A review of continental kingship is provided by Dom H. Leclercq, "Sacre Impériale et Royal," in: *Dictionnaire D'Archéologie Chretienne et De Liturgie,* (Paris, 1950) 15: pp. 304–343. The English rite and its significance is discussed by Leopold G. W. Legg, *English Coronation Records* (Westminster, 1901), in which the *Liber Regalis* is contained, pp. 81–130. William Maskell, *Monumenta Ritualia Ecclesiae Anglicanae* (London, 1847) 3: chap. I discusses the English rite in detail. More directly applicable to the reign of Elizabeth I are J. W. Legg, "The Sacring of the English Kings," *Archaeol. Jour.* 5 (1894): pp. 28–42; H. A. Wilson, "The English Coronation Orders," *Jour. Theol. Studies* 2 (1901): pp. 481–503; and C. G. Bayne, "The Coronation of Queen Elizabeth," *English Hist. Rev.* 22 (1907): pp. 650–673. J. E. Neale in his introduction to *The Quenes Maiesties Passage through the Citie of London to Westminster,* ed., James M. Osborn (New Haven, 1960), argues that such pamphlets as this show the regime's use of the press for propaganda purposes. The edition of the pamphlet used below is contained in A. F. Pollard, *Tudor Tracts, 1532–1588* (New York, 1964), pp. 367–392.

[2] Pollard, *Tudor Tracts,* p. 368; see also J. E. Neale, *Queen Elizabeth I* (Garden City, 1957), pp. 59–63.

[3] Pollard, *Tudor Tracts,* pp. 368–377.

[4] Pollard, *Tudor Tracts,* p. 378.

implicit in the two types of commonwealths portrayed and would displace the barrenness of the one with the plenty of the other.

The lessons of the fourth pageant were borne home to all through the recitation of the causes of good and evil societies. Want of the fear of God, disobedience to rulers, blindness of guides, bribery in magistrates, rebellion in subjects, civil disagreement, flattering of princes, unmercifulness in princes, and unthankfulness in subjects invariably destroyed a commonwealth. Conversely, fear of God, a wise ruler, learned magistrates, obedience to officers, obedient subjects, lovers of the commonweal, rewarded virtue, and chastened vice created a flourishing commonwealth. In this display, then, historical, moral, religious, and civic elements were drawn together to emphasize the responsibilities and rewards of good princes and faithful subjects. It was hardly surprising, therefore, that at St. Paul's School, Elizabeth found her knowledge and virtues favorably compared to those of a philosopher-king. Yet, at the conduit in Fleet Street, she received her highest encomium.

Under a palm tree rich with fruit sat a queen attired in parliament robes. On either side were arrayed six persons representing the estates of the realm. The central figure was none other than "Deborah, The Judge and Restorer of Israel," taking counsel with her nobles, clergy, and commons for the good of the nation. Lest this delicate tribute to the sovereign not be clearly understood, a child reminded those present how God had sent Deborah as a judge to redress the harms of God's people, and concluded:

A worthy precedent, O worthy Queen! thou hast!
A worthy woman, Judge! a woman sent for Stay!
And the like to us, endure always thou may'st;
Thy loving subjects will, with true hearts and tongues, pray![5]

Well might one remember Deborah indeed: valiant in battle and victorious against God's enemies, just and right in peace and happy and virtuous in a long reign. At the Temple Bar, Elizabeth saw two images of Gogmagog the Albion and Corineus the Briton. These two giants held a table which summarized the lessons of the various pageants. Here, too, a child dressed as a poet gave the City's farewell to Elizabeth. Here the child captured the hopes and prayers of her subjects for a glorious reign:

Farewell! O worthy Queen! and as our hope is sure,
That into Error's place, thou wilt now Truth restore!
So trust we that thou wilt our sovereign Queen endure
And loving Lady stand, from henceforth, evermore![6]

The procession was an electrifying experience for Elizabeth and her people. The pageants had clearly stressed the major concepts of secular interest: unity and concord, the cultivation of public and private virtue, and the characteristics of good commonwealths and wise princes. These ideas provided a fitting prelude to the formal drama of the coronation itself.

2.

Although there were some difficulties in getting the appropriate ecclesiastical officials to participate in the coronation of Elizabeth, the service followed closely that outlined in the *Liber Regalis*.[7] Three major parts of this liturgy illumined the concept of kingship—the actions preliminary to the anointing, the anointing itself, and the crowning and presentation of the regalia. These major parts with their various subsections formed a highly intricate rite that reflected the majestic cosmic dance. Sacred and secular elements were blended into one magnificent effort which symbolized the very essence of regality and of the commonwealth.

According to custom, the clergy proceeded from Westminster Abbey to Westminster Hall, chanting a traditional hymn *Salve Festa Dies,* to receive the queen.[8] They, with the great officers of state, then escorted Elizabeth back to the Abbey for the ceremony of consecration. As the procession from the Tower to Westminster Hall had linked the sovereign and her people together, so that from the Hall to the Abbey united her with the ancient estates of the realm. Within the Abbey, the temporal element still remained important in the Recognition which followed and the resounding response of those assembled, "fiat! fiat! vivat Regina Elizabetha!" With the singing of the anthem, *Firmetur manus tua et exaltetur dextera tua iusticia et iudicium preparacio sedis tue misericordia et ueritas precedent faciem tuam alleluya,* the service imperceptibly but significantly moved to subsume secular components under sacred concepts. The process had begun to place the prince within the divine order of sanctification.[9]

The first invocation asked God's grace upon the ruler that through her His presence would be felt among the people. God was, in the prayer, the visitor of the humble who comforted the people through the Holy Spirit. The themes stated were developed more fully as the liturgy proceeded, and they served as a summation for the preceding processions and for the subsequent sermon and oath which next followed. The provisions of the oath were outlined in general terms in the *Liber Regalis.*

---

[5] Pollard, *Tudor Tracts,* p. 387.
[6] Pollard, *Tudor Tracts,* p. 391.

[7] W. H. Frere, *The English Church in the Reigns of Elizabeth and James I* (London, 1904), pp. 10-12; and J. B. Black, *The Reign of Elizabeth, 1558-1603* (Oxford, 1959), pp. 6-11.
[8] John Strype, *Annals of the Reformation* (Oxford, 1824) 1, 1: pp. 28-31. See also Lambeth MSS Cod. Mss 1075a: The Manner of the Coronation of King Edward the VI . . . To which is added Articles concerning the Coronation of Queen Elizabeth . . (Lambeth Palace Library).
[9] *Liber Regalis seu Ordo Consecrandi Regem Solum . . . E Codice Westmonasteriensi editus* (London, 1870), pp. 1-6.

The format suggested by the rubrics was a series of questions and replies. The first question was to ascertain whether the prince would bestow and preserve the laws and customs given to the people of England by their ancient and godly kings, especially the laws, customs, and liberties granted to the clergy and people by St. Edward, and would so swear. The subsidiary questions were refinements of the general statement to uphold the Confessor's laws. The ruler was asked whether she would use her power to preserve peace and godly concord to the Church, the clergy, and the people. Next she was asked whether she would cause equal and right justice and discretion in mercy and truth to be made in all her judgments. Finally, the officiant asked whether she would hold just laws and customs and would promise to keep and defend those which the people enjoyed, to the honor of God.

In the episcopal admonition which followed, the ruler was asked to pardon the bishops and their churches and to preserve their canonical privileges, due laws, and justice. She was also asked to defend the bishops, abbots, and Church as her progenitors had done. All these promises were then sworn to at the altar. The importance of these preliminary actions was that the secular concerns of kingship were placed within the bounds of God's law. This moral order in England was embodied in the legacy of law received from Edward the Confessor and affected and bound every estate of the realm. It was the solemn obligation of the prince, witnessed in the divine presence, to live according to such rules for the well-being of the people who had acknowledged her legitimacy and to ascend the throne as their head.[10]

With the singing of the *Veni Creator Spiritus*, the ritual moves from the preliminary action to the major one of consecration. This ancient hymn implored the Holy Spirit to enter the souls He created and fill them with supernal grace. The hymn emphasized the inter-relationship of the Spirit, the cosmos, and the faithful. As the finger of God's right hand and His highest gift, the Paraclete was the font of life, love, fire, and spiritual unction, who bestowed the seven-fold gifts of wisdom, understanding, counsel, fortitude, knowledge, piety, and fear of the Lord on the faithful. The hymn asked, therefore, that the Spirit would quicken the believer with the fire of love to strengthen his frail flesh and that, having repelled the ancient enemy, the Spirit would grant the believer peace to know the gift of love in the Trinity.[11]

The *Veni Creator Spiritus* presented the vast activity of God in time and in the cosmos. It was a frame in which the sacring process had to be understood for it brought time past into time present, as stated in the *Te invocamus,* the litany, and the seven penitential psalms which followed. The *Te invocamus,* for example, emphasized the activity of God in sustaining the prince through His providence to the very moment at hand. The prayer asked God to enrich the monarch in grace and truth so that she might gladly receive the supreme government through divine grace, might be protected by the wall of God's mercy, and might thus happily govern her people. The litany and psalms likewise pointed out the dependence of the ruler on God's strength, called to mind the adversities humans were subject to, and prayed God to keep the sovereign in His piety, justice, and sanctity. These prayers, then, carefully narrow the activity of God cosmically and chronologically to the immediate necessities of the ruler who must shortly become an integral link in the chain of being.

The prayers which preceded the anointing once again widened the theological and metaphysical concepts and the historical patterns in which regality must be understood. The sovereign was placed in the hierarchy of creation, sanctification, and redemption, through the sacred drama. The collect *Omnipotens sempiterne Deus creator,* for example, described God as the creator of all things, ruler of angels, king over all kingdoms, and lord of all dominions who worked through His chosen people beginning with Abraham's triumph over his enemies. This theological fact was manifested historically through the manifold victories granted to Moses and Joshua, the exaltation of the humble David to the highest seat of power in the kingdom, the ineffable wisdom and peace which enriched Solomon, and special protection granted to all God's followers through the ages. This divine favor was invoked for the sovereign about to be consecrated, as it had been shown to her ancient types. The gifts of God's blessings sought for Elizabeth were prefigured in the fidelity of Abraham, the clemency of Moses, the fortitude of Joshua, the humility of David, and the wisdom of Solomon. Through the blessings of God, the monarch would nourish the Church and people, administer the divine rule of virtue, and shape her people in the harmony of peace and faith. So fortified by God's grace, the prince would overcome all her enemies as Christ, the glory of the humble, through His crucifixion had destroyed Hell and, having overcome the Devil, ascended victoriously to Heaven. The prince according to this collect, then, was the embodiment of the historical action of God prefigured in the children of Israel and was also an embodiment of Christ who was the ultimate paradigm of the obedient victorious ruler.

These central themes were developed further in the collects *Benedic domine hunc Regem, Deus ineffabilis auctor,* and *Deus quo populis virtute* which followed. Using the examples of Davidic authority and the peaceful government of Solomon, the prayer *Benedic domine*

---

[10] *Liber Regalis*, pp. 6–7.

[11] *Liber Regalis*, p. 8. The hymn, *Veni Creator Spiritus,* with commentary appears in Dom Matthew Britt, O.S.B., *The Hymns of the Breviary and Missal* (New York, 1955), pp. 153–157.

sought the same blessings for Elizabeth so that she would be happy in ruling her people, possess a prosperous country, have a long life, and attain God's glory in the eternal kingdom with joy and righteousness. Reminding all that God the framer of the world and creator of all men selected in each age an appropriate ruler from Abraham's bosom, the *Deus ineffabilis auctor* asked God to enrich the queen. God was implored to visit the ruler as uniquely and distinctively as when He had come to Moses in the bush, Joshua in battle, Gideon in the field, and Samuel in the temple. Specifically, God's grace emerged in the imagery of the warrior. He was the hauberk against the attacks of Elizabeth's enemies, a helmet in times of adversity, and an eternal shield of protection in times of prosperity. Ultimately, the divine blessing would bind the people together in the joy of eternity. Finally, the collect *Deus qui populis* stressed the spiritual blessings of God upon the prince for the service of the faith. The God of all virtue and love was requested to endow the prince with the spirit of wisdom and the knowledge of government, so that spiritual rather than temporal results would obtain. Thus, as a ruler devoted wholeheartedly to God, the queen would always be trustworthy in governing the kingdom, and with such divine assistance to a ruler so inclined, the Church would be secure and strong for all time and the Christian faith would continue in tranquility.[12]

From the *Veni Creator Spiritus* to the conclusion of the *Deus qui populis*, the liturgical actions and formulae were intended to place the monarch ever more closely to the center point where terrestrial and celestial converge. The cosmic activity of the Spirit was channeled toward the prince. The secular and sacred nature of kingship was demonstrated historically through the types of the old dispensation, and it was now to be united once more in the queen about to be consecrated. Past time was summoned to bear witness to present time and to augur future time, through liturgical action. The gradual subsuming and transforming of the profane into the sacred reached its finest expression in the salutation, *Sursum corda, gratias agamus,* and the *Vere dignum et justum est* immediately prior to the anointing.

The proper preface transmuted the regal, temporal themes of the prayers into sacerdotal, sacramental ones. It was very meet and right, just and salutary for the faithful always and everywhere to give thanks to God, the strength of the elect and the exaltation of the humble. In the beginning through the outpouring of the Flood, God had chosen to drive out the sins of the world and through a dove carrying an olive branch He had signified the restoration of peace to the earth. Again, He had ordained Aaron a priest by the anointing of oil and had afterward by this ointment perfected priests, kings, and prophets to govern the people of Israel; and, finally, He had foretold through the prophetic voice of David that the Church would be made cheerful by oil. The collect then requested God that by the richness of the oil He would deign to sanctify the sovereign, make her in the likeness of the dove responsible for the peace of her people. The final hope was that the monarch would diligently imitate the example of Aaron in serving God, would attain perfection of government through knowledgeable counsel, would attain judgments by equity, and would achieve a joyful countenance through the unction of oil. Thus, kingly power was integrated into sacerdotal power. The symbols of the flood, the dove, and oil pointed out the concepts of regeneration, sanctification, and transformation applied to the chosen vessel of God. Aaronic priesthood and Davidic kingship were united historically and sacramentally by means of sacred oil. The priestly and kingly characters typologically developed in the prayer were mediated through Hebrew and Christian history and were now immediately applicable to Elizabeth. The act of anointing then followed.[13]

The formulae of the anointing emphasized that these actions were like those used for the ancient prophets and kings, exemplified in Samuel's anointing of David as king. Their purpose was to show that the prince would be blessed and constituted a ruler over her God-given people. Likewise, the anthem sung at this time illustrated the meaning of consecration:

Unxerunt Salomonem Sadoc sacerdos et Nathan propheta regem et accedentes leti dixerunt vivat rex, vivat rex. Vivat rex in eternum. *Ps.* domine in virtute tua let [abitur] rex.[14]

And the actions of Zadok the priest and Nathan the prophet were linked in the prayer, *Prospice omnipotens Deus serenis,* with the similar blessings bestowed on Abraham, Isaac, and Jacob. These were now requested for the prince, namely, the dew of heaven, the fatness of the earth, abundance of corn, wine, and oil with the fruits of God's goodness. Through the prince, these blessings would be a sound country, a peaceful kingdom, and a glorious kingly estate. The ruler herself would be a valiant protector of her people, a consoler of the Church, triumphant over rebels and infidels, amiable and loving to her nobles and people. Finally, she would have children to rule over the realm and attain eternal felicity. The allusions of the anointing formulae, the anthem, and the prayer linked the present ruler with the historical tradition of the ancient kings of Israel as symbols of promise and with the fruition of kingly rule, eternal life.

After the anointing, two prayers, *Deus Dei Filius Jesus Christus* and *Deus qui es justorum,* summarized what had happened. They shifted the typology from

---

[12] *Liber Regalis,* pp. 9–10.
[13] *Liber Regalis,* p. 11.
[14] *Liber Regalis,* p. 12.

the old covenant to the new one. In the first prayer, Christ as the Son of God, exalted above His comrades by the anointing with oil, was implored to send the blessing of the Paraclete upon the prince's head and have it enter her very heart. By this visible gift, the sovereign would receive invisible grace and, having ruled the kingdom justly, woud then reign eternally with Christ who alone was without sin and was King of Kings. Through the anointment, the prince was united with Christ the exemplar of all rulers and the fulfiller of all government. The second collect continued the Christological metaphor. Christ was the glory of the righteous and the mercy of sinners. His attributes set forth the responsibilities and attainment of earthly monarchs for the essence of regal power was seen in the actions of God in redeeming mankind through the sacrifice of His Son, in ending wars, and in sustaining those who trusted Him. God should bless temporal princes who trusted Him, and they in turn should defend the Church and govern with justice and equity. The crown, therefore, with which God crowned monarchs was one of justice and piety. Nevertheless, the highest virtue as seen in Christ was the attainment of love, the love of God's grace symbolized in the holy oil used to anoint kings, priests, and prophets. Proper government of men here and the culmination of joy in heaven were the signs of this love for earthly princes.[15]

The consecration of the monarch was the high point in the liturgical drama. The intricacy of the action and the elaborate recitation of prayers and formulae expressed the intimate connection of the celestial sources of regal power and their temporal embodiments mediated through the office of the king. The great cosmic dance sustained by the Spirit was re-enacted in the anointing rite. The divine blessings imparted to ancient kings and priests were here imparted to the queen. Through visible actions, God's grace is bestowed to transmute the earthly vessel into a fit celestial one. Always at the center, the prince assumed a fixed place through chrism in the chain of being. The prince in the literal and metaphorical senses was the continuation of the royal line of David. Moreover, she was a reflection and reproduction of Christ. Her connection with Him and His with the Davidic and Aaronic tradition united all time in one present moment and person. Finally, the anointing equipped the prince with the necessary public and private virtues of office and showed the objectives of regal power, the glorification of God. As a result of God's action, the prince emerged from the consecration as a *persona mixta,* a divine and human person. The ceremonies which followed this consecration, therefore, struck a clear balance between thoughts and hopes addressed to God and visible signs and firm declarations addressed to the sovereign. The major emphasis centered on the purposes of civil government within the divine economy enuniciated in the anointing. The vesting ceremony, the crowning, and the presentation of the regalia were the manifestations of the basic concepts. Within the liturgical setting, the link between prince and people was finally dramatized by the homage and fealty of the prelates and peers.

The vesting of the monarch which now occurred, according to the rubrics of the *Liber Regalis,* symbolized the ornaments of a good life and holy actions in the prince, and these garments had the aura of sacerdotal power around them. The presentation of the sword by the bishops in virtue of their apostolic authority emphasized the responsibilities of the ruler to defend the Church, widows and orphans, and all other servants of God. As a representative of Christ, the queen had the duty to exercise equity, destroy iniquity, protect the Church against heretics and unbelievers, and, in general, maintain justice and good order. Once the vesting was completed, the crowning occurred and the ring was presented. Both of these actions, like the preliminaries to the anointing, were surrounded with intricate liturgical action and vivid imagery which emphasized the divine character of temporal authority. The prayer for the blessing of the crown, *Deus tuorum corona fidelium,* underscored this theme. God the crown of the faithful was invoked to sanctify the earthly crown, that as it was adorned with precious stones, so would its wearer be filled with graces and virtues. The implications of this imagery were explicitly stated in the formula recited at the moment of coronation:

Coronet te deus corona glorie atque iustitie, honore et opere fortitudinis ut per officium nostre benedictionis cum fide recta et multiplici bonorum operum fructu ad coronam peruenias regni perpetui ipso largiente cuius regnum permanet in secula seculorum.[16]

Together with the prayer and psalm that followed, this statement underscored the dependence of the monarch on God as the Good Shepherd, the loving relationship that obtained between the Almighty and the prince, and called to mind the image of Christ as the servant and master of the people.

The prayer and the formula at the presentation of the ring suggested many rich trinitarian images and historical allusions of God's power. God was the creator who wrote His good law in the hearts of the faithful with His finger, Jesus Christ. Moreover, the Finger of God could never be resisted as the example of the Egyptian magicians illustrated. Moses' triumph over these sorcerers was a prefigure of God's action in a Christian context. God, therefore, was asked to send the Paraclete to bless the royal ring that it would remain a pure metal as it had been created by Him and would be preserved from the infection of the poisoned serpent. The historical and cosmological work of the Spirit was then particularized to the specific royal

---

[15] *Liber Regalis,* pp. 12–13.

[16] *Liber Regalis,* p. 16.

ring and its wearer. The seven-fold gifts of the Spirit were called down upon the queen that she might be sealed with the ring of faith, preserved from sin, and given all the blessings mentioned in the scriptures. The purpose of this request was that whatsoever the ruler sanctified would be made holy, whatsoever she blessed would be blessed. The ring then became a symbol of the Catholic faith and its presentation was a reminder of her obligation to defend that religion so that she might reign at last with the King of Kings.[17]

The worldly and spiritual virtues noted in the liturgy were reiterated with the presentation of the remainder of the regalia. Furthermore, the Hebrew and Christian elements in regal authority were also emphasized. For example, the presentation of the rod showed the Davidic and Christly nature of royal power. As a sign of virtue and equity, the rod could be used by the prince to terrify the wicked. Like David and Christ, Elizabeth had to put down the proud and exalt the humble. Christ was the Door through whom all would enter or be barred. As the Key of David and the Scepter of Israel, He opened and no one closed, He closed and no one opened, and He led the captive out of prison where he sat in the shadow of death. This same Christ should be the prince's aid and support, and the queen His follower. Indeed, David had spoken of Christ as the exemplar whose scepter was the right one, who loved righteousness and hated iniquity, and who by oil was anointed and raised above others. Christ and His attributes served as the most fitting example for an earthly ruler to emulate.[18]

Lawfully sworn, solemnly consecrated, and properly vested, the prince could grant the kiss of peace to the bishops, hear a final episcopal admonition and receive the homage and fealty of prelates and peers. The majestic *Te Deum laudamus* gathered up and comprehended the entire liturgical dance. The eternal frame of order found expression with the lofty praise of the Trinity. Celestial and terrestrial creatures were united in their praise of the Divine Essence and showed their dependence on Him. The orders of angels and humans bowed before the Almighty in a magnificent interplay of macrocosm and microcosm. The praises of prophets, apostles, matryrs, and all the faithful heavenward directed and their acts of faith earthward shown united sacred and secular history. The actions of God, as Father, Son, and Spirit, recalled the eternal themes of sin and redemption, order and chaos. The prayers of the faithful for liberation from sin and for the hope of salvation showed the interconnection of earthy mutability and eternal bliss. The grand concepts were immediately relevant to the monarch, Elizabeth, who was admonished to stand fast and hold to the place she had inherited from her forefathers by the authority of God and by the hands of His servants the bishops. As Christ was the Mediator between God and man, so the sovereign had to be the mediator between clergy and people in order to reign eternally with Christ. As the instrument of the divine will on earth properly prepared, the prince could now receive the homage of the people. In her sacred and secular were finally united, she was the necessary link between the celestial and terrestrial orders. The great cosmic dance which had begun with a temporal action and had moved to sacred spheres, had returned once more to earth through the person of the prince.[19]

3.

In the coronation mass that immediately followed the sacring rite, the epistle and gospel explicated the nature of kingship. Taken from I Peter ii. 13–19, the epistle stressed that all should submit to all human ordinances whether they were from the king or were from any magistrate, because these officials were sent from God to punish evildoers. Liberty, therefore, should not be used as a cloak for license. The faithful ought to honor all men, love the brotherhood, fear God, and honor the king. Such behavior was thankworthy in the sight of God. In the Gospel of Matthew xxii. 15–21, the Petrine exhortation was reinforced. Now the very words of Christ on the nature of temporal authority were set forth, "render therefore unto Caesar the things which are Caesar's; and unto God the things that are God's" (xxii 21, AV). Both clear and ambiguous, this formula captured the essence of the royal mystique proclaimed by the Church, and with the epistle it provided an attempt to articulate the concepts embodied in the drama of consecration.[20]

Buttressed by the scriptures and sustained by the sacramental action of the Church, the doctrine of the prince as developed in the coronation service had the highest theological and moral sanctions available. This proclamation and presentation of regality could not but impress all with the majesty of God manifest in His anointed. With these sanctions were historical, juridical, and political concepts which were integrated into an elaborate liturgical rite for the glorification of God. Moreover, these sanctions and ideas formed an infinite set of correspondences and an elaborate chain of being centered in the prince.

From a juridical perspective, the prince was the legatee and trustee of the laws and customs of the realm, especially the inheritance of Edward the Confessor. Upon the sovereign fell the dread responsibility for their faithful execution and maintenance for the health of the kingdom and of the Church. The solemn promises given in the coronation oath reflected this fact and witnessed this assumption of responsibility. Furthermore, the duties of the monarch prescribed by and fulfilled under the law of the realm were but a part of

---

[17] *Liber Regalis*, pp. 17–18.
[18] *Liber Regalis*, pp. 18–19.
[19] *Liber Regalis*, pp. 19–20.
[20] *Liber Regalis*, pp. 22–30.

the wider obligation to enforce and uphold the law of God which transcended any given kingdom, symbolized in the anointing ceremony.

Understood theologically, the queen emerged as a mediator between God and the people. Her anointing had transformed her into a *persona mixta* who partook of sacred and profane natures like Christ. She was both a dispenser and a receptacle of God's grace and love like the Paraclete. Between celestial and terrestrial, between the communities of saints and angels and that of mortal men, she was an indispensable link. To her, therefore, fell the task of perfecting theological and practical virtues in herself and in her people, so that all could attain the joys of paradise. She was the living embodiment of the two covenants, Hebraic and Christian.

The political facet of the doctrine was expressed in the presentation of the regalia and in the homage of the peers. The prince had the responsibility to maintain law and order. She had to administer justice with equity and mercy, ward off physical and spiritual enemies of her people, and encourage a prosperous realm. Hers was the obligation to set a fitting moral example, to elicit loyalty and devotion, and to protect the Church and people from false and pernicious doctrine. To achieve these ends, the prince had to surround herself with wise, prudent, and devout advisers and officials.

In a historical focus, the ruler was the continuation not only of the ancient royal line of England but also of ancient Israel. Edward the Confessor as well as Joshua, David, and Solomon were her forebears and examples. Hers was the tradition of David and Aaron and of York and Lancaster.

While the Protestant cast of the London pageants might see Elizabeth as a Deborah and underscore the scriptural basis of temporal authority and while the Catholic coronation might portray the queen as a David and stress the sacramental origin of her power, both emphasized her centrality in the divine economy. At the center of the unfolding drama, she commanded the respect, obedience, loyalty, and love of her subjects. Both the pageants and consecration rite emphasized such responsibilities from subjects as ordained of God and necessary for eternal felicity and earthly prosperity. For this intricate ceremony acted out the reciprocal obligations owed the prince by the people, owed the people by the prince, and owed to God by the prince and people, within the frame of order and degree. The stability and seemliness of these concepts offered many opportunities for statesmen and ecclesiastics to use them for their own purposes in the development of a coherent official doctrine of the prince. It is the development of these themes, explored in the coronation festivities, as understood by churchmen and statesmen which must now be examined.

II. DEFENDER OF THE FAITH

As an integral part of the constitutional structure of England, the Church contributed to the development of the royal mystique through its liturgical and homiletical efforts. *The Book of Common Prayer* and the numerous occasional forms of worship that were used throughout the realm contained suffrages, collects, and metrical thanksgivings which set forth the Church's conception of kingship in easily understandable terms. These liturgical works, with the stately coronation ritual, contributed to the creation of a sense of devotion to the queen as the instrument of God's will on earth.

The homiletical efforts of the Church took two forms. One was a collection of sermons—*The Book of Homilies*—appointed to be read regularly in all churches of the kingdom. Second, there were innumerable sermons preached by particular bishops on various occasions. Both categories of sermon literature contained works appropriate to the topic of kingship. "An exhortation concerning good order and obedience to Rulers and Magistrates" in the *Book of Homilies* proclaimed the official doctrine of obedience. Its central theme was elaborated upon by the Elizabethan prelates who, as occasion demanded, took to the pulpit to remind subjects of the nature and function of the office of the prince in the commonwealth.

This chapter analyzes the Church's concept of the prince which augmented that of the *Liber Regalis* and was set forth by authority in public and private liturgical forms, and in sermons preached by men who held sees under Elizabeth. The chapter included a consideration of the liturgical works, sermons preached before the queen at court, and, finally, sermons preached on various occasions and before divers audiences. To avoid many complex historical problems beyond the scope of this study the more strictly polemical and theological works of the prelates have been excluded. A selective method of sermon analysis has been employed since no pretense to exhaustiveness is intended.

1.

The English litany, first used in the Queen's Chapel at Whitehall on January 1, 1559, contained several petitions beseeching the Almighty to look with favor upon the whole Church and the queen. These petitions afford an insight into a basic theme of the liturgical services promulgated during the reign:

That it may please thee to keep and strengthen in the true worshipping of thee, in righteousness and holiness of life, thy servant Elizabeth, our most gracious Queen and governour....

That it may please thee to rule her heart in thy faith, fear and love, and that she may evermore have affiance in thee, and ever seek thy honour and glory....

That it may please thee to be her defender and keeper, giving her the victory over all her enemies.[1]

[1] William K. Clay, ed., *Liturgical Services, Liturgies, and Occasional Forms of Prayer set forth in the Reign of Queen*

The blessing of God's Spirit is also sought for bishops, nobles, and all others in positions of authority that grace, wisdom, and truth may prosper in the realm. The summary of intentions of the faithful is cogently expressed in one of the concluding collects which follow the litany proper. In this collect, the whole course of the queen's life is properly placed in a spiritual context that ultimately envisions the felicity of heaven:

> most heartily we beseech thee with thy favour to behold our most gracious sovereign Lady Queen Elizabeth, and so replenish her with the grace of thy holy Spirit, that she may always incline to thy will, and walk in thy way. Induc [sic] her plentifully with heavenly gifts: Grant her in health and wealth long to live, strength [sic] her that she may vanquish and overcome all her enemies and finally after this life, she may attain everlasting joy and felicity.[2]

These sentiments are incorporated, with slight variations, into the forms of the *Book of Common Prayer* issued in 1559. The petitions contained in the above litany are also in the Prayer Book litany, which was appointed to be used on Sundays, Wednesdays, and Fridays throughout the year. The litanies which were included in the forms for the ordering of deacons, priests, and bishops also memorialized the queen.[3] Such daily offices as Morning and Evening Prayer had several terse suffrages that united the queen and people together in a prayer for God's mercy.[4] While the remembrance of the queen was included in the prayer offices of the Church, "the Order for the Administration of the Lord's Supper, or the Holy Communion" also provided for the invocation of God's blessing in the Prayer of the Church. Here the whole range of human needs and desires is eloquently set forth. As God was asked to unite all men in the truth of His word, He was further petitioned:

> to save and defend all Christian Kings, Princes, and Governours, and especially thy servant Elizabeth our Queen, that under her we may be godly and quietly governed: and grant unto her whole council, and to all that be put in authority under her, that they may truly and indifferently minister justice to the punishment of wickedness and vice, and to the maintenance of God's true religion and virtue.[5]

Thus the formal liturgy of the Church emphasized the moral responsibility of the prince and her people to walk in the light of God's word. Each estate as a part of the Church was presented, and, hence, the obligation of each to fulfill its allotted task was always viewed in the context of eternal salvation.

Supplementing the regular services of the Church were both a series of special prayers and forms of worship pertinent to some momentous national event. Such a form of prayer to be used after the normal litany prayers was issued in 1562. This prayer invoked divine protection upon those English troops serving the cause of true religion in foreign lands. For England, her sovereign, and for those other regions that confessed the gospel, the petitioners desired "perfect peace, quietness, and security" to enable them to magnify God's name.[6] The occasion for the inclusion of petitions for foreigners was the dispatch of English forces to help the French Huguenots.[7] The desire for the triumph of the true gospel, however, was not the sole concern of the Elizabethan prayers. The rising of the northern earls in 1569 caused many to try to understand God's will in this nefarious business. "A Thanksgiving for the suppression of the last rebellion" gave some insights into the relation of God to the body politic.

God, who was the defender of those that put their trust in Him, had visited the realm with "the terror and danger of rebellion, thereby to awake us out of our dead sleep of careless security" which was the result of disobedience and rebellion against the word of God. Nevertheless, by giving the victory to the queen, "her true nobility, and faithful subjects" with little shedding of blood, God had turned this wicked deed to the profit of all men. Thus, the petitioners requested that they might learn by this experience to walk in God's commandments, "and that we, being warned by this thy fatherly correction, do provoke thy just wrath against us no more; but may enjoy the continuance of thy great mercies towards us."[8]

Following immediately upon the rebellion in the North was the St. Bartholomew's Day massacre in France, August 24, 1572. By order of the queen, a special form of Common Prayer was issued on October 27, 1572. The structure of this office was similar to that of Morning Prayer, yet it had a decidedly penitential tone. Among other items, the litany, a collect in time of war, and confessional prayers were ordered. The only joyful note was "A thanksgiving and prayer for the preservation of the Queen, and the Realm." The prayer rendered thanks for the preservation of the queen to date and then asked that God would pardon them for their wickedness so that "thy servant our sovereign Lady, and we thy people ... may by thy protection be continually preserved from all deceits and violences of enemies, and from all other dangers and evils both bodily and ghostly." On this serious note, the rest of the Order is constructed. Prayers were provided to teach subjects to fear God's

---

Elizabeth (Cambridge, The Parker Society, 1847), pp. 12–13. Hereinafter cited as *Public Prayers*. See also, Edward O. Smith, Jr., "The Royal Mystique and Elizabethan Liturgy," *Hist. Mag.* 31: pp. 243–254.

[2] *Public Prayers*, p. 16.
[3] *Public Prayers*, pp. 69–71, 76, 277.
[4] *Public Prayers*, p. 62.
[5] *Public Prayers*, p. 186.

[6] *Public Prayers*, p. 476.
[7] *Public Prayers*, p. 458.
[8] *Public Prayers*, pp. 538–539.

justice and ask for his mercy against further calamities.[9]

Threats of rebellion against the order and stability of a well-governed commonwealth were not the only things that demanded the attention of the Church. The frustrated plot of William Parry in 1585 and the abortive Babington plot of 1586 produced respectively an order for a general thanksgiving in the diocese of Winchester and an order for a general thanksgiving to be used in the province of Canterbury. The Order supplied for the diocese of Winchester by Bishop Cooper required a sermon on the duty of obedience. This sermon was to emphasize "what a grievous and heinous thing it is both before God and man traitorously to seek their [Princes'] destruction and the shedding of their blood, which are the Anointed of God."[10] In the Prayer for the Queen that concluded the Order, the composer rehearsed the heavenly benefits that God had bestowed upon the English Church under Elizabeth and thanked God for sparing her life. "For assuredly if thou hadst not been now on our side . . . the whole floods and waves of wickedness had overwhelmed us, and we had sunk into the bottomless pit of infinite and unspeakable miseries." All must learn to feel the hand of God's justice that "set to sale for money the innocent blood of thine anointed Princes, which thou hast prepared and set up, to be the nurses and protectors of thy truth." The picture of a desolate commonwealth without its anointed queen surely reminded the petitioners of the prophet Daniel's vision and encouraged them to thank God for sparing them from such a calamity.[11]

The Order set forth for the province of Canterbury in 1586 echoed the same thoughts in a more subdued tone. Yet, the point that God directly governs his fatihful sovereigns and subjects is unmistakable.[12] The emphasis on an orderly government of godly princes who ruled by the protection of God is repeated again and again in the various special forms of services for the preservation of the realm from the Spanish invaders which appeared intermittently throughout the 1580's and 1590's.[13]

One significant form of public worship was added to the calendar of Holy Days in 1576. In that year, "A Form of Prayer with Thanks Giving, to be used every year, the 17th of November, being the day of the Queen's Majesty's entry to her reign" was issued by the royal printer. Two years later, this form was re-issued with metrical hymns extolling the benefits of Elizabeth's reign. These thanksgivings were to be sung as psalms.[14] The structure of the order followed that of Morning Prayer. Of special interest was the selection of the first or Old Testament lessons. These called to mind the beneficent rulers of ancient Israel. The second or New Testament lesson was from St. Paul's Epistle to the Romans xiii. With its reading the hearers were duly impressed with the relation of subject and sovereign:

Let every soul be subject unto the higher powers. For there is no power but of God: the powers that be are ordained of God.
Whosoever, therefore, resisteth the power, resisteth the ordinance of God: and they that resist shall receive to themselves damnation. (Rom.xiii. 1–2.A.V.)

This bulwark of monarchy was further reinforced in the Collect for the Queen, which extolled the benefits of a well-ordered commonwealth under the hand of God:

O Lord God, most merciful Father, who as upon this day, placing thy servant our Sovereign and gracious Queen Elizabeth in the kingdom, did deliver thy people of England from danger of war and oppression, both of bodies by tyranny, and of conscience by superstition, restoring peace and true religion, with liberty both of bodies and minds, and hast continued the same thy blessings, without all desert on our part. . . ,

the petitioners asked God to continue these blessings and keep all men in due obedience.[15]

The whole service was mirrored in the metrical thanksgivings which were appended to the 1578 form. A sample of their sentiment can be seen in the following anthem to be sung after Evening Prayer:

Like as thy grace our Queen hath sent,
So bless her rule and government,
Thy glory chiefly to maintain,
And grant her long and prosperous Reign:
All foes confound, and Rebels eke,
That Prince or Church's harm would seek.
  Save, Lord, and bless with good increase
  Thy Church, our Queen and Realm in peace.[16]

The public forms extolling the prince were complemented in the various forms of private prayer set forth by authority. *The Primer* of 1559 contained an Order for Morning Prayer, to be used daily, and a litany which contained prayers and suffrages comparable to those in the *Book of Common Prayer*.[17] *A Book of Christian Prayers, Collected out of the Ancient Writers* appeared in 1578, in which numerous prayers, accompanied by a litany, were given for the private edification of the subject. The scope of these prayers ranges from "A Prayer for the whole Realm, and the body of the Church, with the members thereof, according to their estates and degrees," to "A Prayer for the Queen's majesty."[18] The former contains a fine summary of

---

[9] *Public Prayers*, pp. 544–545.
[10] *Public Prayers*, p. 583.
[11] *Public Prayers*, p. 585.
[12] *Public Prayers*, pp. 597–599.
[13] *Public Prayers*, pp. 608–688.
[14] J. E. Neale, *Essays in Elizabethan History* (New York, 1958), pp. 12–13.
[15] *Public Prayers*, p. 556 f.
[16] *Public Prayers*, p. 560.
[17] William K. Clay, ed., *Private Prayers, Put forth by authority during the Reign of Queen Elizabeth* (Cambridge, The Parker Society, 1851), pp. 14, 53.
[18] Additional prayers appear on pp. 438, 458, 462, 475, 477, 479, 482, 553.

the aims of godly government and the several functions of the subjects. The petitioner entreated God to bring all men together in the knowledge of the truth. Then, he implored divine guidance for rulers so that God would keep princes faithful in their duties of judging and understanding their subjects in the following way:

And forasmuch as thou hast commanded us to pray especially for kings and princes, and for all such as are set in authority, that the company of mankind may live peaceably and quietly under them in all godliness and honesty, considering how burthensome crowns and sceptres are, and how hard the wielding of them is, and how difficult a matter it is to discharge them well, whether it be in respect of themselves, or of their subjects.

In order to further just government, God was asked to remove unfaithful and dissembling counsellors from around the throne and ". . . that all they, whom thou hast put under their charge, may yield them their due and rightful obedience, so as there may be a good and holy union between the head and the members, and thereby it may be known to all men, that the states of all kingdoms and government of all commonweals depend upon thee alone. . . ." Finally, the concluding portions requested God to prevent the evil things that might befall the realm, such as plagues, wars, rebellion, and the like.[19]

The importance of these private prayers is that they set forth not only pious petitions but also theological and political ideas that would greatly influence a devout subject. The total impact of these forms and those of a more public character would be hard to assess. Yet, it would be reasonable to conclude that they form a terse formulation of the prevailing official view of princely government. One other part of the Church's liturgical contribution is the *Book of Homilies,* for this work reflected the collective experience of the ecclesiastical officials in matters of faith and morals, including political morality. This collection of sermons, based on those of the reign of Edward VI, was reprinted and augmented during the reign of Elizabeth.[20] The most important one for our purpose, which appeared in the the 1574 edition, was first entitled "An Exhortation concerning good order and obedience to Rulers and Magistrates." This sermon is vital because it formed the core of the official Elizabethan teaching on the nature of the prince, and served as a model for the variations of emphasis that can be found in the sermons preached by various members of the episcopal bench.

2.

The first part of the Sermon on Obedience in the *Book of Homilies* contains the broad bases on which the official doctrine of kingship rests. God has created all things in an excellent and perfect order. The heavenly hierarchy of angelic power has its counterpart in the earthly hierarchy of kings, princes, and lesser magistrates. As God has appointed an order for the beasts of the earth and has arranged the various members of man's body, such as speech, soul, and the like, in good harmony, so has He assigned to every person his respective place in the social hierarchy. All these correspondences of order, place, and degree point out one unmistakable lesson: nothing can endure or last without the goodly order of God.

For where there is no ryght order, there raigneth all abuse, carnall libertie, enormitie, sinne, and Babylonicall confusion. Take away kinges, Princes, Rulers, Magistrates, Judges . . . no man shall ride or goe by the high way unrobbed . . . all thynges shalbe in common, and there must needes folow al mischiefe and utter destruction both of soules, bodyes, goodes, and common wealthes.[21]

Fortunately, England has been spared this sort of calamity under Elizabeth. Each subject is enjoined to obey, from the bottom of his heart, the laws and proceedings of constituted authority.

Obedience to princes is a commandment of holy scripture, for therein it is stated that all authority is from God and by Him do princes exercise their jurisdiction. Therefore, the obligation of princes and their officers is to gain the requisite knowledge and wisdom necessary to govern their people. It is important to state that princely authority is not derived from the bishop of Rome, "but immediately of GOD moste highest." Since the structure of power is divinely ordained, subjects are not to take private action against others, such as killing, stealing, and the like. Instead, subjects must submit all judgment to God and His princes who bear the sword in his stead, as St. Paul pointed out in his Epistle to the Romans xiii.

This chapter has some other pertinent points. Paul has reminded his hearers that no one, lay or cleric, is exempt from the jurisdiction of princes. External submission to princes is not the only requirement. The individual has to view his obligation as a matter of conscience. "And the same Saint Paul threatenth no less payne, then euerlasting damnation to all disobedient persons, to all resisters agaynste this generall and common aucthoritie . . . ," for such resistance is against God Himself.[22]

The second part of the Homily is more specific in its application. The principle of obedience must extend to all rulers even if they be evil. This premise is supported by the teaching of St. Paul and the example of Christ Himself when He submitted to the jurisdiction of Pilate. Here the sermon stresses that ultimately all civil power is from God, even if it is abused by wicked men. The example of David in his refusal to slay King

---

[19] *Private Prayers,* pp. 458–462.
[20] Alfred Hart, *Shakespeare and the Homilies* (Melbourne, 1934), pp. 20–22.

[21] *Certaine Sermons appoynted by the Queenes Maiestie, to be delcared and readde, . . .* (London, 1574, sig. J4. Hereinafter cited as *Homilies.*
[22] *Homilies,* sig. J4.

Saul further confirms the general rule "to all subjects in the world, not to withstand their liege lord and king, not to take a sword by their private authority against . . . God's anointed, who only beareth and sworde by God's authority for the maintenance of the good and for the punishment of evil."[23]

The above prohibition against active resistance to the monarch has a qualification in the doctrine of passive obedience:

Yet let us believe undoubtedly . . . that we may not obey Kings, Magistrates, or any other . . . if they could command us to do anything contrary to God's commandments. In such a case we ought to say . . . we must rather obey God than man. But nevertheless in that case we may not in any wise withstand violently, or rebel against rulers, or make insurrection, sedition, or tumults . . . against the anointed of the Lord. . . . But we must in such case patiently suffer all wrongs and injuries, referring the judgment of our cause only to God.[24]

For subjects cannot overlook the dreadful punishment of God on those who rebel.

The third part of the homily rehearses the injunctions against treason, and then carries the discussion to the problem of the relation of ecclesiastical officials to the crown. It is emphasized that the numerous scriptural citations cannot in any way be used to support the supremacy of the bishops of Rome over monarchs. The jurisdiction which they claim is a usurped one that is contrary to the teachings of scripture, as set forth by Christ and St. Peter himself. By their example, subjects ought to render tribute to princes. The weight of New Testament teaching is that obedience to princes is for the Lord's sake. "Thus we learne by the woorde of God, to yielde to our king, that is due to our king, that is, honour, obedience, payments of due taxes, customes, tributes, subsidies, loue, and feare."[25] This is the solemn obligation of every subject. Finally, the subject is exhorted, in accordance with St. Paul's teachings, to pray for all men, particularly kings and all that are in authority, that God will favor and protect them, and that these rulers will always have God before their eyes to remind them of their duty. The subject ought to entreat God to grant rulers wisdom, clemency, strength, and zeal so that they may rightly administer justice and defend the true Catholic faith.

The Homily on Obedience carefully shows the harmony of God's universe and how this order is maintained in the body politic. Therefore, to fulfill the law of God, subjects must obey constituted authority. Rebellion is the most heinous crime against the commonwealth because it disturbs the divinely established political order and ultimately threatens to corrupt the very order of nature. Obedience must be rendered to all lawful authority. Even if the prince is evil he must not be resisted. While one may refuse to carry out evil commandments, one may not actively resist. Evil rulers must be borne with patience and understanding. The spbject is further asked to pray for all in authority, that they may understand the will of God in political matters. Finally, to perform his proper function in the order of society, the subject must render the customary tribute and subsidies to the prince. By giving the necessary tribute, the subject is helping to advance the peace and prosperity of the realm.

3.

Sermons preached before the queen at court often centered around texts that the preacher deemed applicable to the pressing problems facing the commonwealth. The emphasis generally seemed to be on the moral responsibilities of the several estates to the total advancement of commonwealth. The regulation of the national life could be properly understood only in the light of Christian morality as embodied in the teachings of the reformed Church of England. In this respect, the following sermons amplify the themes previously discussed in the Homily on Obedience.

In a sermon delivered at Greenwich, Richard Curteys, bishop of Chichester (1570–1582)[26] and a popular court preacher, called attention to Solomon's reflections on youth and old age and their application to the Christian life. One must remember the mercies of God in his youth before he grows old and perfectly serve God while he is still vigorous. For sickness and death are God's bailiffs to remind one of his duty, which is seen in a social context.[27] The grace of God has planted the vineyard of his church, fenced it around with his sacraments, removed idle superstitions, set watchmen as preachers to guard it, and "hathe made a Wine presse of Princes, Judges, and Magistrates. The grace and mercy of God hath set ouer his people godly Kings and Queens, godly Preachers and Ministers."[28] If we fail God, He will curse our doings. It is imperative then to remember that God has saved England from foreign bondage, delivered the Church from the "Romish Pharao," and generally preserved the estates from many calamities.[29] Not only has God preserved the realm, He has also prospered it with material blessings and good government. "Hee hath made a wine

---

[23] *Homilies*, sig. K3.
[24] *Homilies*, sig. K4.
[25] *Homilies*, sig. K4.

[26] The dates given cover the period in which each bishop held his last see under Elizabeth. However, the sermons do not necessarily date from these periods. For the relevant materials, see Edward O. Smith, Jr., "The Elizabethan Doctrine of the Prince as reflected in the Sermons of the Episcopacy, 1559–1603," *Huntington Libr. Quart.* 28 (1964): pp. 1–18; and also, "The Doctrine of the Prince and the Elizabethan Episcopal Sermon," *Anglican Theol. Rev.* 45 (1963): pp. 3–12.
[27] Richard Curteys, *A Sermon Presched at Greenwiche, . . . the 14 Day of March, 1573* (London, 1586), sig. A4, 5 [S.T.C. 6138]. Cited as *Greenwich*.
[28] *Greenwich*, sig. B2.
[29] *Greenwich*, sig. B5.

presse of Judges, Justices, and Magistrates, to presse the huske of contruersies and suites from the iuice, vice from vertue, falsehood from trueth."[30]

Despite these benefits, the people, like the Israelites, have forgotten God. All the blessings afforded them are attributed to their own wits. To this sad situation the preacher addressed a stern warning that, as the fig tree does not leave its sweetness; the olive, its fatness; the vine, its wine; "neyther shoulde wee leave the sweetness of unitie, the fatnesse and substance of religion, the wine of obedience, which doe please both God and man, and be carried away with the bramblees and infidelitie and confusion."[31] All, particularly those in authority, should walk in a spiritual way, for each must render an account of his works on the last day.[32] As Curteys suggested in another sermon, each estate must help the other perform its respective calling.[33] To his mind, the commonwealth is like a fence. It is tied together with fear of God, obedience to the prince, and mutual love one to another. The posts correspond to the nobility, the rails to the clergy, and the pales to the people. By avoiding error and dissensions, the people can be led, like the children of Israel, out of the land of bondage.[34]

Sounding a warning against the inconstancy of the people, John Whitgift, archibishop of Canterbury (1583–1604), delivered a sermon at Greenwich based upon the account of the feeding of the 5,000 recorded in St. John's gospel. The preacher noted the inconstancy of the people, which was caused by their present commodity and pleasure, their emotion rather than reason, and their lack of sound reason and knowledge. Moreover, the people were prone to flattery. This second point had serious implications, "for, if a man in some congregations commend the magistrates and such as be in authority, if he exhort to obedience, if he move unto peace, if he confirm the rites and orders by public authority established," he would endure all sorts of abuse. If such a man attacked or sniped at those in authority or publicly ordained services, then he had achieved many friends. This maliciousness led to two serious consequences, "disobedience to the magistrate, and flat anarchy."[35]

The third vice that beset the people was curiosity. This led to contention. It was this spirit of contention that had invaded the Church of England. As a result certain matters had been called into question. Can a magistrate punish other than by the "judicials of Moses"? Must one obey a magistrate for the sake of conscience? Finally, it was questioned "whether the magistrate may prescribe any kind of apparel to the minister, without doing unto him some injury; which is too, too much to strengthen the authority of the magistrate."[36] The lesson learned from these vices was that one in authority must not seek after popular fame or listen to flatterers. Those who held ecclesiastical posts must be warned that this flattery would lead them from the truth and promote pride and arrogancy, the root of all schism and heresy. The civil magistrates had also to avoid flattery. "For it breedeth in them ambition, the root of rebellion and treason. It moveth them not to be content with their state and calling, but to aspire to greater dignity, and to take those things in hand which commonly turn to their ruin and destruction."[37]

The final message to all his listeners was that they had to remember "we are but strangers in this world and we must behave ourselves as though in a strange country, who though they provide for things necessary for a time, yet their desire and intent is to return home to their own natural country again."[38]

Sermons by John Jewel, bishop of Salisbury (1560–1571), reiterated themes similar to those of Whitgift. While the archbishop emphasized the dangerous vices that beset a commonwealth, Jewel appealed for humility in the Church and commonwealth. The specific application of this principle of humility was presented in the bishop's second sermon, in which he set forth the responsibility of the magistrate to the Church. Reminding his hearers of the destruction of Jerusalem and God's commandment to the prophet Haggai to rebuild the city, Jewel presented this theme as analogous to the present sad state of the Church of England. If the bishops failed to reform the Church, then the prince had to carry out the reform. "For the prince is keeper of the law of God, and that of both tables, as well of the first, that pertaineth to religion, as of the second, that pertaineth to good order; for he is the head of the people, not only of the commons and laity, but also of the ministers and clergy."[39]

Since the prince had the responsibility of reforming the Church by the command of the scriptures and by ancient practice, the claims of the bishop of Rome to superiority over kings and princes were spurious. The Roman claims, from Jewel's point of view, were repugnant to Christ, to sound reason, and to the practice of the primitive Church. One note of caution concluded his sermon. To avoid the destruction of the contemporary Jerusalem, his hearers must not be de-

---

[30] *Greenwich*, sig. B5.
[31] *Greenwich*, sig. C3–D5.
[32] *Greenwich*, sig. D–D3.
[33] Richard Curteys, *A Sermon Presched Before the Queenes Majesty at Richmond* ... (London, 1575), sig. C2, 3 [S.T.C. 6139]. Cited as *Richmond*.
[34] *Richmond*, sig. C4–D.
[35] John Whitgift, *A Godly Sermon Preached before the Queenes Majesty at Greenwich, 1574*, in: *The Works of*, ed., John Ayre (Cambridge, The Parker Society, 1851–1853) 3: p. 572. Cited below as *Whitgift*.

[36] *Whitgift* 3: p. 576.
[37] *Whitgift* 3: p. 579.
[38] *Whitgift* 3: p. 585.
[39] *The Works of John Jewel*, ed., John Ayre (Cambridge, The Parker Society, 1845–1850) 2: p. 996.

ceived by the many false ideas of the day, as were the ancient Israelites.[40]

The enthusiastic conversion of the individual to the love of Christ was a major theme in the sermon preached before the queen by Edwin Sandys, archbishop of York (1575/6–1588). Taking his text from Philippians ii. 2–5, the preacher in the first sermon reminded his hearers of St. Paul's exhortation to brotherly concord and love. Unity in religion and affection is the central theme of the discourse. The archbishop was exceedingly thankful, he said, for the unity of the Church of England in the substance of the gospel, the solid foundation on which the Church is built. Therefore, he deeply regretted the minor disagreements over rites and ceremonies. Existing rites and ceremonies were acceptable as long as these rites did not detract from the preaching of the gospel. He cautioned his audience to beware of those who would hide behind such quibbles, in the guise of reformers, to despoil the patrimony of the Church.[41]

To Sandys, the unity in religion had important consequences for the commonwealth. Unity in religion produced mutual affection between men. This same love in the mystical body of Christ could best be illustrated by a comparison of unity in the natural body. As there was diversity of members in a body so there was diversity of functions.

The prince is as the head, without whose discreet and wise government the laws would cease, and, the people being not ruled by order of laws, ruin and confusion would soon follow.... The ministers of the word are as the eyes to watch, and not to wink or sleep, and as the mouth to speak, and not be dumb.... They are placed as watchmen over the church, for the good and godly direction thereof.... The judges are the ears ... to hear the causes and complaints of the people.... The nobility are as the shoulders and arms to bear the burden of the commonwealth, to hold up the head, and defend the body with might and force, with wise counsel and good advice. Men of lower degrees are set as inferior parts ... painfully to travail for the necessary sustentation both of themselves and others.... This necessary conjunction should cause the prince to love the people.... It should cause such love in the people towards the prince.... Finally, this should cause all men to walk in love.[42]

By avoiding vain-glory and contention, the people could preserve unity by humbleness of mind. However, this sense of humility did not deprive the magistrate of his sword or the minister of his rod to punish sin, but did impose the burden of punishment and the duty of loving the sinner. Thus, the principle of conduct for the commonwealth was the maintenance of concord through caring for others. Such a principle was binding on all, including princes, priests, and counsellors. This principle of conduct "must teach every member to travail for the benefit of the whole body, that the glory of God may be sought of all."[43]

Both Sandys and Gervase Babington, bishop of Worcester (1597–1610), stressed the moral imperatives that guided both prince and people. Magistrates, like Naaman, must seek out the prophetic counsel and heed it if disease were to be prevented in the body politic. Subjects must avoid caviling and carping. Obedience to rulers was the Divine imperative for them. Rulers seeking grave counsel must reform and redress the less than perfect commonwealth.[44]

"Teach us so to number our dayes, that we may applie our hearts unto wisdome," was the text selected by Anthony Rudd, bishop of St. David's (1594–1614/15), when he preached at Richmond, in 1596. The twelfth verse of Psalm 90 afforded the prelate an opportunity to put his hearers, and especially the queen, in mind of the end of their sojourn on earth. To the preacher, the Psalm showed that man had to be taught about the things of God. Therefore, God had provided all ages with great teachers to catechize men.[45] Christians would be better prepared to face the difficulties of this life if they deeply considered the shortness, frailty, and uncertainty of this life, "which is lent unto us for the setting foorth of Gods glorie in it: and withal, in daily meditating how and which way wee may in euery part of our life best profite the Church and commonwealth ... shewing our selues throughout most zealous for the aduancing of Religion and Justice."[46] Hence, each was called to move one another to love and good works. As we grow older, we should become more concerned with spiritual things.

The queen herself at this present reverend age must also give herself to wisdom and private meditation. The preacher then suggested a prayer for the queen, which amounted to a *confiteor*. Elizabeth must entreat God not to remember her sins but of His mercy remember her. "Wherefore lest the Zion and Ierusalem that is, the Church and Commonwealth of England, should be in daunger of thy wrath, through my former sinnes: wash me thoroughly from mine iniquitie, and cleanse me from my sinne."[47] The queen, it was suggested, should thank God for His deliverance from her foreign and domestic enemies, and pray that she might lead a spiritual life here and enjoy life eternal. Finally, "for my subjects' sake let me still be a candle to them

---

[40] *Jewel* 2: p. 997. For additional sermon passages on the authority of the prince to reform the Church and the prince's responsibility for the maintenance of learning in the realm, see also pp. 1014–1015, 1022, 1095–1096.

[41] *The Sermons of Edwin Sandys*, ed., John Ayre (Cambridge, The Parker Society, 1842), pp. 93–95.

[42] *Sandys*, pp. 99–100.

[43] *Sandys*, pp. 103–111.

[44] *Sandys*, pp. 112–113, 120–122. See also Gervase Babington, *A Sermon preached at the Court at Greenwich, the Foure and twentieth Day of May, 1591*, in: *The Works of* ... (London, 1622), pp. 289–296.

[45] Anthony Rudd, *A Sermon preached at Richmond before queene Elizabeth upon the 28 of March 1596* (London, 1603), pp. 1–10 [S.T.C. 21432].

[46] Rudd, p. 13.

[47] Rudd, p. 50.

a little longer until the state is established for times to come so that after my departure, they may live in peace and plenty in the future age. So at length I may go to the selpulchers of my fathers, like David, in a good age full of dayes, riches, and honour." [48]

These sermons preached at court had two major threads of thought. One stressed the public aspect of kingship while the other stressed the private aspect. The public theme developed around the concept of the commonwealth as a unity comparable to a body. In this body, there were several estates that had specific functions and duties to perform for the well-being of the whole. The prince had a particular responsibility to reform and govern the Church according to the word of God. The authority of the prince in the eccelesiastical area as in the temporal area was derived directly from God, as the scriptures taught. Therefore, subjects were commanded to obey the prince in all matters. Only if the prince commanded an act that was counter to the law of God could a subject refuse to obey. However, in refusing obedience to authority, the subject must willingly submit to punishment. Rebellion or active resistance was strictly prohibited. Positively stated, this argument meant that each subject must actively fulfill his respective station and thereby assist in furthering good government and true religion.

The private aspect of the sermons emphasized the development of the spiritual life of the individual, especially the prince's life. Each was urged to follow the example of Christ by actively practicing humility and love of his neighbor. For the prince such a religious commitment required meditation, prayer, and the study of God's word. Spiritual regeneration would show in the administration of justice with mercy, and the deep concern for the spiritual and temporal welfare of the prince's subjects. Only through the spiritual regeneration of the individual could the commonwealth flourish and testify to the blessings of God.

4.

The national religious festival of the Accession Day became part of the Church's calendar by 1576 and was the occasion for much merry-making and joyous thanksgiving. The intensity of allegiance to the queen and the religious devotion that surrounded the seventeenth of November is reflected in the following three sermons. The first two were delivered by archbishop Sandys at York on the same day. If one can judge from the first sermon, both were probably preached in 1579.[49] The third sermon was preached by the archbishop of Canterbury, John Whitgift, at St. Paul's, London, in 1583. All three sermons emphasize the obligations of Christian sovereigns and subjects.

Solemn assemblies were ordained in the Church to commemorate special occasions to thank God for His blessings, such as the passover and feast of the tabernacles. England has had great cause to rejoice because God has given the realm a gracious sovereign who has restored religion and liberty to the people. So the preacher's text, Canticles ii. 15, "Take us the little foxes which destroy the vines: for our vine hath flourished," recalled the mercies of God to the people and the people's duties to God and their enemies. The vineyard of England, the Church, has now been properly blessed with a wise, learned, and religious overseer.[50]

If learning and wisdom be so necessarily required in a governor, how great is the goodness of Almighty God to us-ward, which hath so plentifully bestowed this gift of knowledge and wisdom upon our sovereign, not inferior to Mithridates for diversity of languages, but far surmounting all former English princes in learning, knowledge and understanding which rare and excellent gift dwelleth not in her royal breast alone, but is beautified and accompanied with sundry other most singular graves. She is the very patroness of true religion, rightly termed "the Defender of the Faith"; one that before all other things seeketh the kingdom of God.[51]

The queen has always desired to have men appointed who would administer justice fairly and show mercy to all. With such a queen as her governor, the Church has been purged from idolatry and superstition. Under Elizabeth's guidance, the word of God has been properly preached and the sacraments rightly administered. The fencing of the Church with good laws has brought civil peace and plenty. England has become a land of milk and honey.[52]

Despite all the good work of the queen, little foxes—heretics, atheists, and others—have sought to destroy the vineyard by every conceivable device. Therefore, these foxes should be reconciled with the Church by the minister and magistrate. The minister by preaching, godly conversation, and good example must attempt to capture them. If these devices failed, he must use ecclesiastical discipline. The magistrate must also try to remove the foxes by the trap of the law. The lawful means for Christian magistrates were death, exile, confiscation, and incarceration. "Thus, it is the duty as well of the magistrate as the minister to obey the commandment of the Almighty, and by all means to present wicked enterprises, to root out evil, and to seek the safety of God's vineyard, his beloved church."[53]

Sandys's second sermon was based on St. Paul's injunction to Timothy that we should pray for all men, particularly kings and all in authority. The archbishop reminded his audience that the observance of the Accession was comparable to the observance by the Children of Israel of their deliverance out of Egypt. For under Elizabeth, the English have been delivered from the

---

[48] *Rudd*, p. 55.
[49] *Sandys*, p. 56.
[50] *Sandys*, pp. 55–57.
[51] *Sandys*, p. 57.
[52] *Sandys*, pp. 58–61.
[53] *Sandys*, p. 74.

bondage of Rome. The exhortation of the apostle to pray for princes had a specific purpose.

In exhorting us to pray he sheweth the benefit and fruit of our prayer. We must pray to God to give us good princes and rulers: under a good prince we ought to lead a good life: a good prince should procure peace, piety, and honesty to the people: a good people should live peaceably, godly, and honestly under their prince.[54]

The command of St. Paul required all to pray for both good and evil princes. One should pray that God would turn the heart of an evil prince, and one should praise God for a good prince. "We ought daily and hourly to pour out supplications, that God would grant them a long life, a safe government, a sure dwelling, valiant soldiers, faithful counsellors, a good people . . . and whatsoever the hearts of men or kings do desire."[55] The English have been well blessed with their good and gracious sovereign Elizabeth, their Judith, Deborah, and Esther. For God has blessed the work of her hands. She was indeed the model prince.

In summation, Sandys urged his listeners to pray that God would bless the realm with faithful ministers of the word who would proclaim their message fearlessly. He also exhorted his congregation to pray that magistrates be wise and just, that they obey the laws themselves, and show no partiality in administering them to others. Finally, he called upon all men to lead a holy life expressed through the public duties of prayer, hearing the word of God, and worthily receiving the sacrament.[56]

The archbishop of Canterbury invited his hearers to consider the third chapter of St. Paul's Epistle to Titus as a suitable text for the occasion. Men were told to be subject to principalities and powers and to be obedient to magistrates. For obedience was commanded of God. "The magistrate is appointed by God. He is his vicar and vicegerent. He giveth them his name and title, . . . 'I said, ye are gods' "[57] Obedience was also required since all power is of God. Therefore, whether the prince was good or evil, he must be obeyed.

The magistrate should encourage the righteous and punish the wicked. Thus, if there was no magistrate, there would be no surety of goods or life. Everything would be subject to spoliation and the weak would be oppressed by the strong. Therefore, it might be better to have a tyrant than no king at all. A kingdom without a king was like a choir without a chanter. Following this line of thought, Whitgift reminded his hearers that disobedience was punished with a short life in this world or with eternal punishment in the life hereafter.[58]

Obedience consisted of doing, praying, and honoring. By the idea of doing, the preacher suggested that, while many gave lip service to the magistrate, they did not in fact truly obey him. To the question, "Must one obey the magistrate in all things?" Whitgift replied that the commandments of magistrates which were not against the word of God bound men in conscience and must be kept upon pain of damnation. If commanded to do anything contrary to the word of God, one must answer with the apostle that it was better to obey God than man.

The second part of obedience was praying. The apostle enjoined all men to pray for those in authority. Such a commandment rebuffed those who criticized the assemblies and meetings held to commemorate the Accession. The third part of obedience was honor, which consisted of love and fear in one's external action and in the inner heart. Where love and fear existed, commonwealths prosper, flourish, and increase. Against these three parts of obedience, there were three groups that exemplified disobedience—the papists, anabaptists, and wayward and conceited persons. The anabaptists erred in their desire to abolish all authority, while the papists erred in seeking to qualify the conditions under which magistrates can exercise authority. Yet in the Church of England authority was given to the magistrate in causes ecclesiastical. This did not mean that the magistrate thereby performed ecclesiastical functions as preaching, administering the sacraments, and consecrating bishops, as some imagined. The function of the magistrate was to see that all subjects obey, honor, and serve God. For princes have both tables of the commandments committed to their charge.[59]

"The third sort are those wayward and conceited fellows who do not 'condemn' magistrates, but 'contemn' [i.e., scorn] and despise magistrates. These men will obey, but it is what they list, whom they list, and wherein they list themselves. And all because they cannot be governed themselves."[60] This group outwardly showed godliness, yet they were not ashamed to speak ill of those in authority. In brief, they were slanderers and evil speakers who produced contention. While most men were prone to criticize bishops and magistrates, all men should have been aware that the devil was the cause of this mischief. He sought to undermine the spread of the word of God by such attacks. Therefore, all should watch out for those who hid their attacks in the guise of religion, perfection, and faith. For all must realize the punishments involved for spreaders of contention and the dangers involved to the commonwealth. In conclusion, the preacher felt that it was far better to enjoy the blessings that accrued from true obedience to magistrates than to indulge in slander.[61]

---

[54] *Sandys*, p. 76.
[55] *Sandys*, p. 80.
[56] *Sandys*, pp. 82–86.
[57] *Whitgift* 3: pp. 586–587.
[58] *Whitgift* 3: pp. 588–489.

[59] *Whitgift* 3: pp. 590–592.
[60] *Whitgift* 3: pp. 593.
[61] *Whitgift* 3: pp. 593–596.

The festival of the Accession offered the prelates an opportunity to rehearse the blessings that God had bestowed on England under the governance of Elizabeth. Secondly, the preachers were able to paint a picture of an ideal prince, one honest and God-fearing, who preserved the Church from false and pernicious doctrine and administered the laws with equity to all subjects. Finally, the festival permitted the bishops to propound the subjects' duty of obedience to princes, without offering any real qualifications to such unlimited claims. Princes, whether good or evil, were divinely constituted authorities that demanded absolute obedience upon pain of temporal and eternal punishment. Thus, this joyous occasion permitted the promulgation of the official concept of kingship in which the duties of the subject were firmly and enthusiastically hammered home, and the prince was gently reminded of his grave responsibilities to the commonwealth.

5.

London and its environs, as the center of the nation, offered many places and occasions for the outstanding men of the Church to set forth their views on the state of the commonwealth. For example, Westminster Abbey at the opening of Parliament was used to full advantage by the Church. The outdoor public pulpits in London, like St. Mary Spital and Paul's Cross, enabled the government and the Church to present important ideas to large audiences estimated to run as high as 6,000 souls at the latter pulpit.[62] The sitting of a Parliament or the occasion of some foreign event deemed important to the government or the queen, such as the death of a friendly king, would permit an opportunity for an outstanding prelate to present an appropriate message. Outside of the nation's capital, the bishops would find the summoning of the local assizes, a visit to one of the universities, or the normal duty of preaching in their own cathedrals suitable occasions for the treating of matters of civil and religious interest that presented the doctrine of kingship to the auditors, in one form or another. Some of the sermons used on these occasions are presented below to show further the extensive effort made to establish an official concept of kingship throughout England.

In "A Sermon Made before the Parliament at Westminster," delivered on April 2, 1571,[63] Edwin Sandys directed the attention of his audience to the relation between God, the prince, and the people. Good princes have always held consultations for the reformation and preservation of the commonwealth, in which three things must be considered: the state of religion, the state of the prince, and the state of the commonwealth. "If religion be not sound, men's souls cannot be safe: if the head be not preserved, the body of necessity must decay: If good government want, the commonwealth falleth into confusion."[64] Citing the example of Samuel, Sandys indicated that the queen was now following this ancient pattern of the prophet and the Israelites.

Like Samuel, the magistrate must be faithful and upright and ought not to be resisted. He must also be zealous in the matters of religion and the affairs of the commonwealth. Thus, Samuel was a model of the mild and zealous prince. The text enabled the preacher to comment upon the function of the minister to the prince. The preacher must pray for prince and people and teach the word of God. Should he fail to do this, the prince had a duty to remove him.[65]

While Sandys did not advocate bloodshed, he observed, "that the maintainers and teachers of errors and heresy are to be repressed in every Christian commonwealth. Such troublers of the quiet of the church, such deceivers of the people, are at least wise, according to the ancient commendable custom of the church, to be removed from the ministry."[66] For if the minister could not pray and teach in the right way, then he must give way to him who would.

Both the prince and the people owed fear and love to God, as sons owed these to their father. Citing Saint Augustine, Sandys suggested that "'the king serveth God as a man one way, and another way as a king; as a man by leading a faithful life; as a king by making laws, such as enjoin things that are just, and forbid the contrary.'"[67] Therefore, the first duty of the prince was to purge the Church from false doctrine and practices. Secondly, the prince must see that the gospel was properly preached. In his relation to the Church, the prince must "see the gospel every where preached, the ministers provided for, and the people compelled to come hear the word . . . of God."[68]

In his responsibilities to the commonwealth, the prince must punish evil and defend the good so that each man might perform his respective duty. As shepherd of his people, he must choose wise and learned counsellors and lesser magistrates who truly fear and seek to serve God. In line with these observations on the nature of princely power, the preacher indicated that the function of a parliament was to bind up the wounds that exist in the commonwealth—diversity of religion, corruption, usury, the needs of the poor—with sound laws. Since law was the life of the commonwealth, statutes that were enacted must be enforced and kept by all. The magistrates had a peculiar respon-

---

[62] Alan F. Herr, *The Elizabethan Sermon: A Survey and Bibliography* (Philadelphia, 1940), p. 24. See also Haddon W. Robinson, "Politics and Preaching in the English Reformation," *Bibliotheca Sacra* 122 (1965): pp. 120–133.

[63] For the date of this sermon, see J. E. Neale, *Elizabeth I and Her Parliaments, 1559–1581* (New York, 1958), p. 185.

[64] *Sandys*, p. 34.
[65] *Sandys*, pp. 36–39.
[66] *Sandys*, p. 40.
[67] *Sandys*, p. 42.
[68] *Sandys*, p. 46.

sibility both to obey and to enforce the law. If the magistrate failed to observe the laws of the realm, one could not expect the subject to obey them.

Thus, to God, all men must render fear and love; to the prince, the anointed of God, all men must render honor for the sake of conscience and subsidies to protect the realm; to the commonwealth, all men must render it safe and peaceable. If subjects and prince labored to correct the abuses in the realm, God will bless their efforts. If men are unfaithful to "our good Samuel, to our gracious sovereign," God will surely destroy all.[69]

At Paul's Cross during the parliament time of 1588, Richard Bancroft, bishop of London (1597–1604),[70] preached a trenchant sermon against the Puritans. Choosing as his text, "Deerly beloved, believe not every spirit, but trie the spirits whether they be of God: For manie false prophets are gone out into the world," (I John iv.1), the bishop proceeded to expose the Puritan menace to the established order of Church and state. As false prophets had always existed in the Church, so did they exist at the present time in England. Chief among these were those who perverted the sayings of scripture to support false doctrines that would replace the existing government of the Church with one modeled after that of the ancient Jewish synagogues. This Puritan discipline would hold all responsible to a general synod as a final arbiter. Such schemes totally disregarded churches, like the English, that performed their functions despite certain blemishes. It seemed strange to the preacher that such a form of government, attributed to Christ, should not have been discovered for 1,500 years![71] Referring to the Martin Marprelate controversies,[72] Bancroft suggested that contempt of bishops, ambition, self-love, and covetousness were the causes of these false prophets. The intent of their scheme was to deprive the Church of its patrimony for the benefit of the few. The bishop defended the Established Church, which attempted to steer a middle course between two unpleasant alternatives of papalism and puritanism. The genius of the Anglican Church was that it held the scriptures in high regard and also relied upon the decisions of councils of bishops to clarify its doctrine and practice. Thus, the locus of authority was public, not private, judgment. Hence, the right to demand subscription to articles of faith of the Church's ministers was a laudable custom in which the civil magistrate concurred.[73]

The attacks against the preaching and sacraments of the Church of England, coupled with the Puritan attack on the *Prayer Book*, could be viewed only as a slander to the queen, since the Puritans desired to substitute their own book and ecclesiastical order for the existing arrangement.

> For woulde you think that in a booke of this nature describing so perfect a platforme of Church government, the civill magistrat should bee quite forgotten? Was there ever untill this daie anie publike confession set foorth by any true church in the world . . . that Kings and Queenes shoulde bee the fosterers and nurses of the church, where any supremacy or government of persons, and in causes ecclesiasticall the civill magistrate is wholie left out? Can there be in a christian common-weal such an absolute order of ecclesiasticall government, as they brag of, set downe for the only forme, which is necessarie to be observed without anie mention of the civill magistrate?[74]

The Puritans also attacked the bishops for having preeminence in dignity and authority over the rest of the clergy. Another point of contention was that the Established Church had replaced a spiritual pope with a temporal pope. Bancroft suggested that the Puritan objection to petty popes—namely the bishops—ought to be carried to its logical conclusion, which would also reject the authority of the civil magistrate in causes ecclesiastical. By the logic of Puritan argument, the queen must also be a petty pope and, therefore, ought to be removed.

Touching the Anglican understanding of the supremacy of the crown, Bishop Bancroft maintained that this supremacy had been returned to the crown from the usurped Roman jurisdiction and, therefore, all causes, both civil and ecclesiastical, had once more been reunited with the crown of England.

> In this supremacie, these principall points were contained: that the king hath ordinarie authoritie in causes ecclesiasticall: that he is the chiefest in the decision and determination of church causes: that he hath ordinarie authoritie for making all lawes, ceremonies, and constitutions are or ought to be of force: and lastly, that al appellations, which before were made to Rome, should ever be made heer after to his Majesties chauncerie to be ended and determined. . . .[75]

The supremacy of the crown ran counter to the Presbyterians' claim that their synods should have such authority. The example of Scotland showed the intentions of this faction. For the situation created by the Presbyterian party in Scotland had resulted in the overthrow of the state and the decay of the crown. Since these Puritans had set themselves above the civil authority, asserted the right of deposition of monarchs, and the right of people to take up arms against their

---

[69] *Sandys*, pp. 49–54.

[70] Richard Bancroft served as archbishop of Canterbury under James I, 1604–1610. Under Elizabeth, his highest preferment was the Bishopric of London.

[71] Richard Bancroft, *A Sermon Preached at Paules Crosse the 9. of Februarie, being the first Sunday in the Parleament, Anno. 1588* (London, 1589), pp. 1–12.

[72] This sermon was part of Bancroft's exposé of the Puritan movement, and it aroused considerable resentment in Scotland. For the Martin Marprelate controversy and related theological issues, see J. B. Black, *The Reign of Elizabeth, 1558–1603* (Oxford, 1959), pp. 201–202; Donld J. McGinn, *John Penry and the Marprelate Controversy* (New Brunswick, 1966); and John F. H. New, *Anglican and Puritan: the Basis of their Opposition, 1558–1640* (Stanford, 1964).

[73] Bancroft, pp. 14–49.
[74] Bancroft, p. 63.
[75] Bancroft, pp. 69–70.

sovereign, they would have perforce suggested that the queen too ought to be removed for maintaining her ecclesiastical supremacy. Therefore, in matters of church government, the Puritans and papists espouse the same doctrine. When they would openly deny the queen's auothrity, the preacher did not know. Yet he suggested that their proposed reformation must be effected without the queen's consent. Such action would clearly be rebellious and deny the queen's negative voice in the making of laws.

In the light of these seditious doctrines, the magistrate must put down such evil-doers, and private men should admonish them and eschew their company. The action proposed by the Puritans, while ostensibly aimed at Church reform would totally upset the commonwealth. To re-emphasize the nefariousness of their actions, Bancroft called his hearers' attention to the results of presbyterian reform in Scotland. All men should be aware that the doctrine of the Church of England was sound and that those who would abolish the existing order sought to subject prince and people to a very popelike tyranny by asserting the supremacy of their presbyteries over all men. Acts of Parliament, civil matters, private morals, and theology would all be subjected to this pretended holy discipline. Having thus exposed the implicit danger in puritanism, the good bishop reminded his hearers of the traditional testimonies that supported the religion established in England.[76]

While continuing the theme of responsibility in the commonwealth, William Overton, bishop of Coventry and Lichfield (1579-1609), approached the matter in another context. Addressing the judges of Sussex, Overton wanted them, the justices of the peace, and jurymen to deal more earnestly in matters of religion than they had been wont to do.[77] Selecting his theme from Romans xvi. 17, the bishop enjoined his audience to take heed of those that caused dissension and gave offense contrary to the doctrine they had received. Just peace grounded upon the true knowledge and fear of God was requisite for all states, public and private. Hence, one should avoid sowers of dissension because they upset and destroyed all things, even the commonwealth.

There were two types of dissension—one spiritual, the other temporal. The preacher maintained that St. Paul in his epistle discussed both types. Addressing these judges and lawyers, Overton stated that the nature of their vocation did not permit them to ignore spiritual dissension. For they could not "shifte off this kind of matter from you, as thoughe it wer a meere alien to your other businesse, but you must also have to do with it aswel as wyth other matters, and may not estrange it from your present affaires. For whom come you to serue, come you not to serue Christ?"[78] While each must serve the prince, he could not do this effectively unless he first served Christ. For "Christ is a patterne unto the Prince, and the Churche is a patterne unto the common wealth to follow. Neyther is that common wealth a good commonwealth, or commendable before God, which doth not frame and conforme it selfe after Christ."[79] As the judges and lawyers were assembled to redress the wounds of the commonwealth, they must also bind up the wounds of the Church, by ending schism and sectarianism that threatened to undo everything. The cause of queen and commonwealth could not be separated from the cause of Christ. Hence, as their commissions charged them, the judges must look into the problem of Puritan and papist sectarianism as well as into those things that disturbed the civil order. For the combination of temporal and religious abuses tended to overthrow law, queen, and commonwealth. Therefore, let each man do his utmost to fulfill his office and remember that he has a duty to serve God and not man only. By serving God and His Church, those assembled would serve the queen and commonwealth well.[80]

A summation of much of the sermon literature was set down in a sermon by Archbishop Sandys, based on the familiar thirteenth chapter of St. Paul's Epistle to the Romans. In this sermon preached at York, the archbishop outlined the obligations of the people to the prince in very emphatic and clear terms. Nor did he overlook the responsibility that a prince and the lesser magistrates owed to the commonwealth.

According to Sandys, the Epistle to the Romans sketched the office and authority of the magistrate and the duty and obedience of subjects to him. From this description, a general and absolute rule could be formulated: that every person without exception owed obedience to the higher powers—namely, to the prince. The first important reason was that all power was derived of God. Therefore, whether the prince was Christian or heathen, good or bad, his authority came from God. Thus, all subjects must obey the magistrate for conscience' sake, for to resist the prince was to resist God and to invoke His judgment. Therefore, resisters and rebels would receive the wrath of God either in this life or in the next.

Other reasons for obedience were that only evil-doers needed fear the sword. The just man need not fear the prince, for the office of the prince consisted partly in repressing evil. Since the prince possessed the sword, subjects ought to remember from whom he held it. The power of the prince must also remind the subject that princely power was not an empty threat. Nevertheless, if magistrates commanded actions against

---

[76] Bancroft, pp. 72-100.
[77] William Overton, *A Godlye and pithie exhortation, made to the judges of Sussex* [12 Feb. 1579] (London, n.d.), sig. A2 [S.T.C. 18925a, Folger Library].
[78] Overton, sig. A5.
[79] Overton, sig. A5.
[80] Overton, sig. B-D5.

the ordinance of God, one must answer that it was better to obey God than man. Because the office of the magistrate was "painful and chargeable," subjects ought to pay tribute to princes, as well as honor and reverence them. For they have been appointed to spend their goods and lives in the interest of the commonwealth by suppressing evil, encouraging virtue, defending their subjects, and governing well. All these things were done by God's ordinance for the subjects' benefit.[81]

On the other hand, the magistrate owed a debt to his people.

The debt of the magistrate is just execution of lawful punishment against transgressors. The sword is delivered unto him for that purpose: neither is any open transgression of any kind, whether it concern the first or second table of the law of God, or any man of any calling be he prophet or priest, exempted from this judgment. . . . It is also a part of the magistrate's debt to give upright sentence in matters of controversy between parties.

Lesser magistrates must be chosen from those who were wise, courageous, religious, and sought the truth. Partiality, excessive affection, undue commiseration, covetousness, and the desire to please men, were undesirable traits in lesser authorities.

All men then must walk in the way of God's truth. The true subject fulfilled the will of God by rendering obedience, fear, honor, tribute, and custom to the magistrate. Dutiful subjects must always remember that God punished those who overtly or covertly resisted the magistrate.[82]

Sandys's sermon summarizes the cardinal points of the clerical position on the nature of kingship. One notes a strong emphasis on the doctrine of obedience, which is based on moral sanctions ordained by God. Conversely, the prince is also morally responsible for his actions. He, too, must fulfill with justice and equity the duties that God has given him. Nevertheless, the problem that remains unsolved is the absence of a practical remedy, should the prince violate the moral order. Sandys's solution of obedience to all constituted authority certainly does not offer a satisfactory answer.

6.

The liturgy of the Church provided a firm foundation upon which the clerical concept of the prince could be erected. For the liturgy brought the teaching of the Church directly to the people in simple terms that could be understood by every subject. The numerous orders of worship, both public and private, addressed the subject at every level of his spiritual life. Thus, the primary contribution of the liturgical forms was their ceaseless repetition of a point of view. Within these services, the subject was constantly taught to pray for the prince. The eloquent language of the Church's prayers reminded subjects that they must desire a just and merciful prince who would follow the precepts of God. For the prince, acting immediately under God, was responsible for the well-governance of the commonwealth. Therefore, each subject must pray for the prince's well-being and cooperate with him in supporting just government. The subject had to be obedient to duly constituted authority, for God would not suffer rebellion to go unpunished.

The terse phrases of the liturgy only fleetingly captured the full doctrine of the prince. However, the Church, in its Homily on Obedience, developed the line of thought implicit in the liturgy. The central theme of this homily was that God had ordained the structure of the existing society, so that all power was derived from God and was delegated to his vicegerent, the prince. Therefore, unqualified obedience—obedience for the sake of conscience—was required of the subject. Only if the prince commanded any action contrary to the law of God, could a subject demur from obeying the ruler. However, such refusal was not construed as license to rebellion or open resistance to constituted authority. The subject must also pray for the prince. If the prince conformed to the law of God, the commonwealth would flourish.

While the Homily on Obedience stressed the obligation of the subject to the prince, the many sermons preached by the prelates expanded the scope of the official doctrine of the prince. The preachers maintained that the prince was given the power to rule in all areas of society. Therefore, the ruler exercised the right to reform the religious establishment and restrain false and contentious doctrines within his realm. However, this did not mean that the prince was ordained by God to perform specifically spiritual functions like preaching. Instead, the prince had to see that the spiritual estate properly performed its assigned functions. The prince also had an obligation to rule the other estates of the realm justly and mercifully. His responsibility was to administer justice to all regardless of their station in life. Therefore, his actions must always conform to the existing laws of the state and to the precepts of God. In the staffing of the lower magistracy, the prince had an obligation to select the best men available and supervise their performances.

The office of the prince then was clearly delimited by the preachers. These men also developed another aspect of the nature of the princely office by setting an outline of desirable personal characteristics for the ruler. The prince should be just and merciful. That is an obvious condition for one vested with power. However, mere exercise of moral virtue was not enough. The prince had to be a deeply devoted Christian. Meditation and prayer, the pursuit of knowledge and the study of God's word, were personal characteristics required of a prince. For the preachers underscored the fact that the prince had an obligation to set an example for others to emulate in their daily lives. Thus, the concept of the

---

[81] *Sandys*, pp. 197–199.
[82] *Sandys*, pp. 200–203.

prince advanced by the prelates included two aspects, a public functional one and a private religious one.

The second important division of the doctrine of the prince as expounded by the bishops pertained to the subject. Each estate of the realm had its particular contribution to make to the well-functioning of the commonwealth. Hence, each order must strive to perform its obligations and encourage others to do likewise. The nobility had to defend the realm and advise the prince; the ministers had to declare God's will to men and denounce evil; and the commons had to support the realm through lawful occupations. While each estate had its peculiar function, all subjects of all estates had two major obligations to the ruler. First, subjects were to obey the prince as far as the law of God allowed. However, this did not give anyone the right to resist the will of a ruler even if his action was immoral. Subjects must bear patiently with evil rulers, not resist them. On the positive side, the subject must support the prince by obediently rendering tribute, honor, and reverence.

The second obligation of all subjects was religious. Each had a duty to pray for the welfare of the prince so that he would rule according to God's will. The subject also had a religious obligation to cultivate the Christian virtues in his own life so that he might be an example to all men and thereby strengthen the commonwealth.

In summation, one might observe two important aspects of the Church's doctrine. First, the doctrine suggested that the existing order of society was the finest expression of God's handiwork and, therefore, must not be altered. The second point is that the teaching of the Church offered no adequate practical solution to the possible abuse of princely power. All estates were forbidden to resist the prince openly. Also, the ruler was solely responsible for his actions, in practice, to God alone. The binding agents were the existing moral order and the will of God. However, one may not infer that this constituted a doctrine of the divine right of kings. For the preachers nowhere suggested that the king was above the moral law, which included the customary law of the realm. For the Elizabethan bishops, the prince was not the source of the law. While their doctrine did not provide for any responsible control of the prince's prerogatives by the people, one must not infer a doctrine of unlimited monarchial power, for the prelates did not ignore the existing constitutional arrangements that were reflected in the High Court of Parliament.

III. PRINCE, PARLIAMENT, AND PEOPLE

Various members of the Elizabethan state contributed to the maintenance of the royal mystique through their development of a doctrine of the prince which was presented for public consumption. The official doctrine was shaped by two major types of material. First, the writings of individual members of highest echelons of government drew upon their intimate knowledge of statecraft to present a concept of the commonwealth which might be termed an apology for the existing order of English society and the policy of Elizabeth's government. Second, the numerous speeches of the queen, delivered to her various parliaments, presented the sovereign's personal conception of her office and helped to project this image to the assembled members and to the realm.

The purpose of this chapter is to examine these materials and then summarize, as far as possible, the composite picture of the prince that emerges. Since many works written by prominent officials are not pertinent for this examination, the names of many distinguished members of the government will not appear. No effort has been made to include such corporate expressions of the royal mystique as acts of Parliament and the Privy Council, proclamations of the realm, the decisions of justices of the courts, or other comparable material which might be classified properly as administrative or judicial, rather than political in character. Finally, the speeches of the queen have been restricted to those presented to the several parliaments during her reign.

1.

Sir Thomas Smith held many important positions in the Elizabethan government. He served as ambassador to France and as a member of the Privy Council. His most important post was that of secretary of state, which he held from 1572 until his death in 1577. His important work, *De Republica Anglorum, The Maner of Governement of England,* was written in English in 1565 and appeared in print for the first time n 1583.[1] In this work, Smith clearly set forth the relation of the prince to the commonwealth. In order to present this idea, Sir Thomas surveyed the entire English constitutional structure.

The author began his study with an analysis of the classic Greek forms of government—monarchy, aristocracy, and democracy. He then discussed the corruptions of these forms—tyranny, oligarchy, and anarchy. Since these latter forms reflected the sickness that mght affect a body politic, Smith continued his presentation of illness in the body politic with a brief discussion of rebellion. Sir Thomas stated the matter in

---

[1] Christopher Morris, *Political Thought in England: Tyndale to Hooker* (London, 1953), p. 81; and *Dict. Natl. Biog.* **18**: pp. 533–534. See also R. W. K. Hinton, "English Constitutional Theories from Sir John Fortescue to Sir John Eliot," *English Hist. Rev.* **75** (1960): pp. 418–421. Arthur B. Ferguson, "The Tudor Commonwealth and the Sense of Change," *Jour. British Studies* **3** (1963): pp. 11–35, shows the integration of concepts of change and progress into the older constructs of "place, order, and degree," and the increasing awareness of the need for positive governmental activity in a dynamic society.

the following way:

> So when the common-wealth is euill gouerned by an euill ruler and uniust ... if the lawes be made, as most like they bee alwaies, to maintaine that estate therefore the question remaineth, whether the obedience of them be just and the disobedience wrong? the profite and conseruation of that estate right and justice, or the dissolution? and whether a good and upright man, and louer of his countrey ought to maintaine and obey them, or seeke by all meanes to abolish them ... which hath been the cause of many commotions in common wealths: whereof the iudgement of the common people is according to the euent and successe: of them which be learned according to the purpose of the dooers, and the estate of the time then present, certaine it is, that it is alwaies a doubtful and hazardous matter to meddle with the changing of lawes and gouernement, or to disobey the orders of the rule on gouernement, which a man doth find already established.[2]

Surely one could not blame him for adroitly avoiding a thorough discussion of so dangerous a topic! Yet, it was significant that Smith did not expressly deny the right of the subject to rebel; nor did he appeal to any theory of natural law or divine right to disapprove of the implicit right of rebellion. His appeal to the opinions of the learned was certainly a pragmatic rather than dogmatic basis for argument. The significance of his discussion was in the unuttered words—in the profound silence and verbal equivocation.

The gingerly handled problem of rebellion gave way to a more forthright exposition of kingship.

> Where one person beareth the rule, they define that to bee the state of a King who by succession or election commeth with the good will of the people to that gouernement, and dooth administer the Commonwealth, by the Lawes of the same, and by equity, and doth seeke the profit of the people as his own.[3]

Smith was averse neither to pointing out the responsibility of kingship in general nor to offering his considered opinion on the absolute administrative power of a prince:

> But as such absolute administration in time of warre when all is in armes, and when lawes hold their peace because they cannot be heard, is most necessary: so in time of peace the same is very dangerous as well as to him that doth use it, and much more to people upon whome it is used: whereof the cause is the frailitie of mans nature, which ... cannot abide or beare long that absolute and uncontrolled authoritie, without swelling into too much pride and insolencie.[4]

Ancient history confirmed, for Smith, the soundness of his observation. These strictures on kingship laid the groundwork for his discussion of the commonwealth of England.

Sir Thomas surveyed all the aspects of English society that would be of value in understanding the operation of its constitution. Crucal in this discussion was his definition of commonwealth:

> A common-wealth is called a societie or Common doing of a multitude of free men, collected together, and united by common accord and couenants among themselves, for the conuersation of themselves, as well in peace as in warre. For properly an Hoast of men is not called a Commonwealth, but abusiuely, because they are collected but for a time, and for a fact: which done each diuideth himselfe from others as they were before.[5]

The commonwealth was not a transitory collection of people. It was an association of people pursuing common objectives: nobles, gentlemen, yeoman, and laborers bound together in common under their prince. Each stratum of society had its particular distinctions, perquisites, and responsibilities. This society, formed by traditions and a common purpose, was reflected in the structure of the High Court of Parliament.

"The most high and abosolute power of the Realme of England consisteth in the parlement."[6] Here, king, nobles, representatives of the Commons, and bishops representing the clergy assembled ". . . to aduertise, consult, and shew what is good and necessarie for the Commonwealth, and to consult together . . ." and, having maturely deliberated, to make laws for the realm. It was understandable then why Parliament was considered absolute, i.e., without higher appeal, for all interested members were represented.

> The Parlement abrogateth old lawes, maketh newe, giueth order for things past, and for things hereafter to be followed, changeth right and possessions of priuate men, legitmateth bastards, establisheth formes of religion, altereth waights and measures, giueth forme of succession to the Crowne, defineth of doubtfull rights, whereof is no law already made, appointeth subsidies, tailes, taxes, and impositions, giueth most free pardons and absolutions, restoreth in blood and name, as the highest court condemneth or absolueth them whome the Prince will put to that triall.[7]

Since the whole realm was present in microcosm, Parliament had the absolute power of the head and body together. Its actions were assumed to have the consent of all Englishmen.

A consideration of the political structure of the realm must inevitably center around the head—the prince. The prince had certain prerogatives that operated independently of the body. Notably he had the right and authority to conduct foreign policy, and the right thereby to declare war and conclude peace. There was one limitation to this prerogative: the prince must act upon the advice of his Privy Council. However, Smith did not suggest that the prince was bound by the advice of the Council. In fact, Smith pointed out that this Council, composed of distinguished members of the nobility and commonality, existed solely in the prince's sufferance.

---

[2] Thomas Smith, *The Commonwealth of England, and the Maner of Gouernement Thereof* (London, 1612), pp. 4–5.
[3] Smith, p. 7.
[4] Smith, p. 7.
[5] Smith, p. 11.
[6] Smith, p. 36.
[7] Smith, p. 37.

Discussing another prerogative power, Smith asserted:

> In warre time, and in the field the Prince hath also absolute power, so that his word is a law, hee may put to death, or to other bodily punishment, whome hee shall thinke so to deserve, without processe of lawe or forme of judgment.[8]

While this absolute power had been exercised within the realm in times of rebellion and insurrection, and prior to declaration of open war, the judgment of "wise and graue men" was against such action. The learned apparently did not like the implications of a prince exercising martial law, if he could proceed within the normal order of the law. Reluctantly, Sir Thomas maintained that such a prerogative must exist in a kingdom to cope with emergencies that did not permit normal recourse to the courts.[9]

The prince had other important prerogatives, such as the regulation of coinage, without need for any consultation with the rest of the realm. His proclamation in such matters was of absolute force. The royal prerogative also extended to mitigation of the law in equity, and the mitigation of punishment for transgressions of the criminal law, "where the paine of the Lawe is applied onely to the Prince."[10] The prerogative of mercy then could not be used to deprive a subject of his just rights when these were established by law. The prince could only remit that which was his own. Smith concluded his description of the role of the prince as follows:

> To bee short, the Prince is the life, the head, and the authoritie of all things that bee done in the Realme of England. And to no Prince is done more honour and reuerence, then to the King and Queene of England: no man speaketh to the Prince, nor serueth at the table, but in adoration and kneeling, all persons of the Realme bee bare-headed before him in so much that in the chamber of presence where the cloath of state is set, no man dare walk, yet though the Prince bee not there, no man dare tarry there but bare headed. This is understood of the subjects of the Realme, for all strangers be suffered there and in all places to use the manner of their country, such is the ciuilitie of our Nation.[11]

In summary, Smith had set forth the basic division of power within the commonwealth. The prince and Parliament shared the responsibility of making laws for the commonwealth and of providing for the maintenance and defense of the realm. The prince alone had the authority in the conduct of foreign policy and in the selection of the principal officers of state and of the magistrates.

Smith's analysis of the constitution of England presented some significant observations concerning the power of the prince. If the commonwealth was formed by a society of free men, one might have legitimately questioned the necessity of having a prince to share in the rule. Smith solved this problem by suggesting that the prince was limited in power. Since the commonwealth was formed by free men, it was safe to infer that they were more than mere goods or property and, therefore, had rights of their own. He suggested the line of demarcation between the rights of the prince and those of his subjects. The true prince was one who ruled by the laws of the commonwealth. Here we see the first limitation on the power of the prince—the common law. This formed the framework within which the prince must operate. Hence, there was a limited sovereign controlled by the customary law of the commonwealth.

The operation of this principle could be seen in the judicial exercise of the royal prerogative. The prince might not tamper with the rights of his subjects, but could only remit his own rights under the law. A second limitation, a legislative one, imposed upon the prince was that he might not tamper with the laws and customs of his subjects without their consent. The prince had absolute power in the selection of his officials and in the conduct of foreign policy. Because the prince also had the duty to defend his subjects in time of war, the emergency power vested in the crown to deploy the national resources as needed and to depart from due process of law was not denied. Yet, Smith was chary of admitting the exercise of such power in time of rebellion.

These theoretical limitations on the prince raised the problem of practical restraints on royal power. On this issue, Smith neither suggested that punishment would be in the next world, nor did he really offer any other alternate solution. For, ". . . it is alwaies a doubtfull and hazardous matter to meddle with the changing of lawes and gouernement, or to disobey the orders of the rule or gouernement, which a man doth find already established."[12]

While neither prince nor people were completely absolute when acting independently, united in Parliament they were absolute, for there was no higher authority. Smith's analysis of the powers of Parliament as representative of the whole realm clearly showed this. Here, each part of the commonwealth could work for the general welfare. But, there was even in this absolutism of the King-in-Parliament the problem of undefined powers of the respective estates. One can conclude that Smith had conceived the power of the prince to be limited by the customs and laws of the realm. But it appears that neither the people in general nor the Lords and Commons in Parliament had any effective control over the exercise of royal power, if the prince violated the constitutional arrangement.[13] At best, the

---

[8] Smith, p. 46.
[9] Smith, p. 47.
[10] Smith, p. 48.
[11] Smith, pp. 49–50.

[12] Smith, p. 5.
[13] George L. Mosse, "Change and Continuity in the Tudor Constitution," *Speculum* 22 (1947): pp. 20–27.

prince had a moral obligation to adhere to established order.

In 1583 William Cecil, Lord Burghley, published *The Execution of Justice in England,* which attempted to justify the queen's policy towards her Catholic subjects. Cecil had held many posts under Elizabeth. His two most important positions were successively that of secretary of state and lord treasurer; the latter he held from 1572 until his death. From his intimate knowledge of statecraft, the lord treasurer was well qualified to present a temperate and balanced argument in defense of the queen's policies, especially as these pertained to the relation of religious conviction and open rebellion. These two problems were intimately tied to the nature and duties of a prince.

For Burghley, all offenders tended to cover their faults with contrary causes, and rebels tried very diligently to cover theirs. At this writing, Cecil maintained, there were those who had previously expressed their allegiance to the queen, but even now were in rebellion in England and Ireland. The rebels' purposes have been:

. . . to haue desposed the Queenes Maiestie from her Crowne, and to haue traiterously set in her place some other whom they liked, whereby if they had not bene speedily resisted, they would haue committed great bloodsheddes and slaughters of her Maiesties faithfull subjects, and ruined their natiue countrey.[14]

Not that these rebels had stopped here. The irony of their action was that they attempted to plead their religion as an excuse and claim that they merely wanted to restore papal jurisdiction. Yet, said Cecil, they had lived notoriously even before the rebellion. The important point from his view was that the queen must maintain order, and in the suppression of these rebellions she acted according to the law.

Despite the lewd character of these rebels, the pope had encouraged them in their nefarious work,

that is, to take armes against their lawefull Queene, to inuade her realme with foreine forces, to pursue al her good subiects and their natiue countries with fire and sworde.[15]

The pope's encouragement has been reinforced with numerous bulls and other writings that denounced the queen as a usurper and called upon her subjects to renounce their "natural alleageances, where-to by birth and by othe they were bounde."[16] Such action by a pastor seemed despicable to Burghley. To further implement this invidious plan, seminary priests have been sent to England to carry out the provisions of the papal bull. Against these foreign and domestic threats, the government has been forced to act, and their manner of action, as Cecil presented it, was significant.

Providentially, God has given the queen wisdom,

. . . whereby she hath caused some of these sedicious deedemen and sowers of rebellion, to be discouered for all their secret lurkings, and to be taken and charged with these former points of high treason, not being delt withall upon questions of religion, but iustly condemned as traitors. At which time, notwithstanding al maner gentle wayes of persuasions used, to moue them to desist from such manifest traiterous determinations.[17]

These trouble-makers have suffered death then not by any new statutes established for religion or against the papal supremacy in ecclesiastical causes, but by the ancient laws of the realm. Burghley referred to the Act of Treasons of 1352.[18] By citing this statute of Edward III, he pointed up the temporal character of the offense and also indicated that such an act had been in effect when the "Bishops of Rome and Popes were suffered to haue their authoritie Ecclesiastical in this realme. . . ."[19]

Those who renounced their treasons have been spared. Yet, foreigners still fomented strife and tried to cloak their malevolence with the guise of religion. Certainly, no one could reasonably deny the duty that the queen and her magistrates owed to God to maintain the peace of the realm. Theirs then was the task of extirpating these villains either by the sword or by the law to prevent the shedding of innocent blood.

And though there are many subiects knownen in the realme, that differ in some opinions of religion from the Church of England, and that doe also not forebeare to professe the same, yet in that they doe also professe loyaltie and obedience to her maiestie, and offer readily in her Maiesties defence to impugne and resist any foreine force [even the Pope], none of these sort are for their contrary opinions in religion prosecuted or charged with any crymes or paines of treason, nor yet willingly searched in their consciences for their contrarie opinions, that sauour not of treason.[20]

The best proof to illustrate Cecil's point that religion was divorced from political treason was that the Marian bishops have not been executed for their beliefs but have remained at liberty as long as they have not engaged in seditious acts. In fact, Burghley was emphatic in pointing out that no one was persecuted for maintaining the pope's supremacy in ecclesiastical causes, and thereby denying the queen's supremacy over ecclesiastical persons in her own realm. Although these opinions ran contrary to certain statutes, no punishment has been meted out for holding these views. The only punishment has been for "those who maintain the contents of the Bull that the Queen is not the rightful ruler of

---

[14] William Cecil, *The Execution of Justice in England for Maintenaunce of Publique and Christian Peace* (London, 1583), sig. A2. The text used is that by Scholars' Facsimiles and Reprints (New York, 1935). An excellent edition of the text with a fine introduction is that prepared for the Folger Shakespeare Library. Robert M. Kingdon, ed., *The Execution of Justice in England . . .* (Ithaca, 1965).

[15] Cecil, sig. A3.

[16] Cecil, sig. A3. The reference is to the bull of Pius V, *regnans in excelsis,* 1570.

[17] Cecil, A3.
[18] 25 Edw. III, st. 5, c. 2.
[19] Cecil, sig. A3.
[20] Cecil, sig. B1.

England, and that here subjects are discharged of their paths of obedience and loyalty." [21]

Burghley concluded his argument by attempting to show that the pope, by arrogating to himself temporal power, exceeded the function of the spiritual order. Since all were subject to higher powers, especially kings, the clerical order was not exempt from this rule.[22] As other princes have maintained their kingdoms free from papal encroachments, so now was Elizabeth pursuing the same policy.[23]

In his tract, Burghley tried to distinguish between religious conviction and rebellion against the prince. Therefore, he carefully asserted the duty of the queen to protect her realms fom domestic rebellion and foreign interference. The queen could fulfill this obligation to God and her subjects only by the use of the sword and by process of law, as particular circumstance warranted. Cecil also maintained that the queen's policies were motivated by a sense of necessity, yet tempered by wisdom and mercy, essential elements in a prince.

It seemed, from the direction of the Lord Treasurer's argument, that he was trying to divorce the temporal policies of government from the crown's supremacy in ecclesiastical causes. In so doing, he carefully pointed out that the queen had no desire to probe into the private religious convictions of her subjects. The government seemed willing to settle for external conformity. Only when religious conviction through treasonable action threatened the established political-religious structure of the commonwealth did the government interfere with "matters of conscience." The burden of his argument had no place for a concept of religious toleration insofar as toleration implied the establishment of other legally recognized religious bodies. However, the matter of private belief, it seemed from Cecil's argument, did lie outside the normal scope of governmental purview.

The moral aspect of the doctrine of the prince is developed by Sir Thomas Wilson in his *A Discourse Upon Usurye*, which appeared in 1572. Sir Thomas had served in several important positions prior to his assuming in 1577 the post of secretary of state, which he held until his death in 1581. While still serving as master of requests, Wilson dedicated his work to Robert Dudley, earl of Leicester, one of Elizabeth's favorite courtiers. Although his specific discussion of usury did not concern the doctrine of the prince, Wilson based it upon certain observations on the nature of society and the role of the magistrate which appeared in a lengthy epistle dedicatory. In his survey of Elizabethan society, Wilson saw a moral decline engendered by poor economic practices. Therefore, he lashed out at the evil of usury, which in his eyes was one of the greatest menaces to the commonwealth. He began his discussion with certain general observations about the order of society and then specifically described the role of the magistrate in this order. One feels that Wilson tried to develop a general philosophy of society which would enable him to relate specific problems— such as usury—to his basic premises. Only by a thorough understanding of the nature of society and its ultimate purpose could the prince effectively govern his dominions and correct specific abuses.

Since the world was made for man and he for God, so that man might have pleasure and God honor, one must do his duty and keep God before his eyes in advancing the cause of religion and in doing justice. The result of both would be the praise of God. Since the Fall men were subject to corruption and not always mindful of their duties, so they must be reminded and warned.[24] With these preliminary remarks, Wilson launched into the heart of his argument.

Wariness in all things was wisdom, advised dealings produced perfection, and things forseen did less harm. For this cause then were laws enacted, that they might punish evil and also prevent its commission. By preventive legislation, men could be warned in advance to live in good order; if they did otherwise, they had the deterrent of the sword to consider.

Wilson then discussed the responsibility of magistrates in the commonwealth, basing the argument on his moral understanding of man's nature and of the function of law:

I doe wish therefore that man were as apte to doe righte, as hee is readie to speake of right, and it be all together, as he would seme to bee: least otherwise lawes stand not in vaine, when great occasion geeues iust cause of speedie redresse. And in thys behalf magistrates are to be put in remembrance, that they hauing gouernement and execucion of iustice in their handes, maye bee good ryghters of all wrong doynges, and iust dispensers of gods lawe, and mans lawe, both to lowe and hyghe, to ryche and poore, without any respecte or regarde of parson. For most true it is, that where iustice is dulie ministred, there is god moste hyghly and sweete is that sacrifice to god, when the lyues of lewde men are offered by to suffer paynes of death for wicked dooynges.[25]

His harshness must not be misunderstood. Wilson was not arguing for the indiscriminate use of capital punishment, nor was he suggesting that perfection could be attained in the commonwealth. He was merely pointing out that of the many abuses in the commonwealth none gave more offense than usury, for it caused great grief and spread mischief. So Wilson felt justified in venting his righteous indignation.

Usury had become widespread throughout England. Wilson felt that this practice was immoral as it trans-

---

[21] Cecil, sig. B2.
[22] Cecil, sig. C3.
[23] Cecil, sig. D3.
[24] Thomas Wilson, *A Discourse upon Usurye* (London, 1572), sig. C2 [S.T.C. 25807]. See also Albert J. Schmidt, "Thomas Wilson and the Tudor Commonwealth: An Essay in Civic Humanism," *Huntington Libr. Quart.* 23 (1959): pp. 49–60.
[25] Wilson, sig. C3.

gressed the law, violated Nature, and derogated God. It replaced charitable dealings with hardness of heart and extortion. This offense was second only to renuciation of God and of his magistrates, and, therefore, very hurtful to the commonwealth. Now men of substance were given to idleness, contrary to God's law. This malaise that plagued society reminded Wilson of the two sorts of man that must be looked on critically: the dissembling gospeller and the willful and obdurate papist. The first group would overthrow all religion, deceive for private gain, undo the commonwealth of men, and did in fact practice usury more than any other group. The second were dangerous to the commonwealth, for they were open blasphemers of the truth. Between the two the world was a prey and God was highly dishonored.

Statesmen such as Leicester must beware of these people, as they followed only for what they could obtain from persons of quality.

Cicero sayethe wiselye, holsome seueritie, doth greatly excede the vayne shewe of folish pitie. Clemencie is good, I deny not, but that is to bee used to good men, or else towardes suche as of whome there is good hope of theire better behauioure hereafter. But where clemencie is altogether abused, and maketh as it were an open waye to all lowsenes in maners and carnall libertie of lyfe, there seueritie must needes stryke a stroke.[26]

Certainly a not too subtle blast at magnanimous Leicester! Yet one cannot help feel that Wilson was aiming higher. His emphasis on excessive clemency might very well refer to the queen herself. If one considered his oblique reference to the tolerant policy towards papist and Puritan, one might be sorely tempted to suggest that his remarks were surely aimed at Elizabeth. He continued:

For the law it selfe, is a dumme magistrate to al men, whereas magistrates are a speakynge lawe to all people. And therefore, as gouernours do submit themselues to lawe, and lyue thereafter: so will the people submitte themselues to gouernours and theire doynges: suche force (lo) hath example of life, especiallie in magistrates.[27]

The point that the magistrate was an example to his people was further reinforced by Wilson. The magistrate was not just a private person. He was also a public figure who had a responsibility to do good for the many who would not or could not care for themselves. It was possible for a magistrate to do good for the people and still offend against himself; or to do good for himself and offend the people. Of these types it was better to offend against oneself and not the people "because the common welfare dependeth uppon their wel doyng."

And good it were also neuer to remitte apparante greate faultes unto any person in authority. For the magistrate abusing hys office, deserueth more punishments than doth the priuate personne. For as hee abuseth hys charge, so doth hee deceaue hys trust, [and] by example geeuethe great cause of much euill.[28]

Nevertheless, this was not to be construed as a justification for anyone to do evil in the hope of hiding his doings from the prince. "For tyme doth discouer all, and god hath graunted thys priuylege unto prynces, that wicked attemptes, shall neuer hauer deepe roote."[29] Ultimately, these nefarious dealings would be revealed to the disgrace of the doer and to prove the justice of God and further His glory.

One other point Wilson wished to stress. It was just as bad not to cherish the good and the godly in a commonwealth as it was to permit the wicked to go unpunished. Therefore, he wished that the preachers might be heeded in their condemnation of usury. Lamentably this was not the case, for the magistrate "doth not ioyne with them, and see that executed by censures of the lawe, which they so earnestly rebuke in the pulpite, and shew foorth gods threates most vehemently, for suche synnes so much suffered and so lyttle punished."[30] To Wilson this was a terrible state of affairs. Usurers were common thieves and ought to be treated as such. Is it any wonder then that he prayed that God would send England a Solon or a Thomas Cromwell to remove this cancer from the body politic?

Wilson's treatise attempted to set the magistrate or prince within the moral order of the universe. By so arguing he was able to appeal for the redress of a grievance in strictly ethical terms. The body politic was an organic whole in which the public official, particularly the prince, must act in the best interest of all. This view permitted Wilson to state that it was better for the magistrate to be immoral in his private conduct than in his public life. By drawing this sharp distinction between the private and public responsibility of the magistrate, the author could lash out against the lack of public morality that had been supported by acquiescent public officials.

In the course of this jeremiad one can sense the indignation of the just against those in high places who abdicated their moral responsibility by failure to enforce existing laws and by failure to remedy evil by statutes. The ultimate judgment was in God's hands. For all government was ultimately under His control and subject finally to His judgment. With this underlying assumption, Wilson could easily point to the misuse of Christian virtues such as clemency. At this point, the author might well cite the laxity in securing religious uniformity so essential to preserving the commonwealth, or chastise the magistrates for their failure to heed the admonitions of the clergy. One feels that Wilson was implying that the magistrate was under moral

---

[26] Wilson, sig. C4.
[27] Wilson, sig. C4.

[28] Wilson, sig. C4.
[29] Wilson, sig. C4.
[30] Wilson, sig. C4.

obligation to heed the "voice of the Lord" when proclaimed from the pulpit.

Clearly, the treatise demonstrated one of the basic assumptions of the period: that the commonwealth was the instrumentality of God through which the moral life was perfected. Hence, the rulers had a grave duty to maintain order and degree so that the common sort could learn by example. Failure to heed the moral strictures of the prophetic voice of preaching ultimately resulted in dire consequences not only for the ruler but for the commonwealth. Wilson's views expressed a moral tone quite in contrast to the more practically oriented Smith and Cecil. Yet, it is to Wilson's credit that he grasped the importance of specific issues, in this case usury, and then tried to relate the universal law of nature to this one issue. For him, the microcosm must always strive to emulate the perfection of God's ultimate design.

The temporal officers of state present a picture of the prince that is based on the existing constitutional structure and provides for the exigencies of policy. Therefore, the arguments presented by Cecil and Smith are pragmatic rather than moral in nature. The prince is limited by the laws and customs of the realm. It is his responsibility to preserve the common law of England. In order to do this, the prince must observe the limitations imposed upon him. Under normal conditions the prince cannot disregard the rights of the subject in legal matters. Therefore, in dispensing and pardoning, the exercise of the royal prerogative must be restricted to the rights of the crown and must not extend to the rights of the subjects. Further, the prince may not alter or abrogate laws and customs without the consent of the people as they are represented in the High Court of Parliament. Thus, the prince is limited in his personal exercise of sovereignty. Only when he is acting with the Parliament is he absolute, for there is no higher judicial or legislative authority than King-in-Parliament.

As the hand of the commonwealth, the prince receives the highest reverence and honor from his subjects. He exercises his prerogative absolutely in certain areas without the interference of others. Foreign policy, the appointment and removal of officials, the coinage, and the emergency war power are his exclusive areas of competence. Nevertheless, the prince has the responsibility of protecting the liberties of his subjects by avoiding excessive use of the prerogative when other customary means of procedure are available. He ought not to suspend the common law unless the commonwealth is threatened with a grave crisis.

In a well-ordered commonwealth, the prince has the duty of preserving peace and warding off rebellion by the use of the sword or by process of law. Since the sovereign can distinguish between the private religious beliefs of his subjects and actions which threaten the public safety, he has to be certain that disaffected subjects do not cloak their treason in a religious guise. While the ruler must punish traitors and rebels, he does not impose religious beliefs upon men's consciences. The prince is satisfied with external conformity to the established religious practices of the realm. By not opening windows into men's souls and by insisting on proper respect for the established religious institutions, the prince can maintain peace and tranquillity within the kingdom. Thus, the needs of men's bodies and souls will be adequately provided for.

To complement the prince's obligations, the subject has his duties. The most important duty is that he refrain from rebellion. The subject must obey constituted authority and refrain from altering the existing structure of society. For each member of the commonwealth must respect the order and degree which exists in society. It is important to point out that neither Smith nor Burghley discusses the moral right of the subject to rebel. To them, it is a matter of policy that subjects obey. Morality is not a consideration.

While Smith and Cecil present a pragmatic argument, Wilson develops a moral one. Society in his view is governed by fixed laws of nature which represent the divine will in the body politic. Since man and society are moral agents and responsible for their actions, the prince has an obligation to redress moral lapses through the swift execution of justice. The prince also has an obligation to provide laws that will prevent future lapses and rigorously enforce the laws by his public actions. While the private life of the prince may not inspire emulation, he must act publicly in such a way that the commonwealth's interests are paramount. By placing the public welfare before his private interest, the prince can provide an example for all to follow. It is significant to note that Wilson does not touch upon the problem of obedience. His argument is concerned with the implementation of princely policy in a peaceful society.

All of the writers agree that the primary duty of the prince—either from a legal or moral view—is to maintain peace and prosperity within the realm. This happy state can be achieved by the formulation and implementation of sound and moderate policies. If the private life of the prince is not virtuous, one can at least expect that he will maintain a sense of public virtue by promoting the best interests of all the estates of the realm. Although the statesmen might appeal to the public with their own views of the nature of the prince, the temporal aspect of the royal mystique found its greatest expositor in the queen herself. While using public ceremonies, pageants, and progresses to great advantage, Elizabeth made her most consummate contribution to the royal romance in her speeches at parliament-time.

2.

The greatest challenge to the queen was the parliamentary stage. Here in view of the whole realm, the actress *par excellence* gave free scope to her talents. Venting stormy wrath or righteous indignation, radiating beneficent sunshine, or wooing her lovers, Elizabeth skillfully dominated the performance with the right word, the proper gesture, and the perfect emotion. Nothing was left to chance. The show ran for forty-three years to the exaltation of one and the edification of all. Marriage, religion, the succession, the Scottish queen, the subsidy, and the queen's safety were the various themes woven into one great drama. One must now look at the speeches the queen delivered—each carefully prepared in advance—each contributing to a picture of the prince.

No sooner had the reign begun than the queen was besieged with petitions to marry and thereby secure the succession. On this matter, as on other important ones, the queen temporized, flattered, cajoled, threatened, and finally won her point. In 1559 the drama started on the theme of marriage. Elizabeth always had considered herself the "servitor of God," and, therefore, trusted that her present mode of life was pleasing to Him. Had not she been pressured to marry during the reign of her sister, and remained constant in her resolution? She liked the manner of the petition of the Commons for they made no attempt to limit the place or person. Yet, if such an effort had been made, the queen would have misliked it and construed it as presumption, "Being unfitting and altogether unmeet for you to require them that may command, or those to appoint whose parts are to desire, or such to bind and limit whose duties are to obey, or to take upon you to draw my love to your liking or frame my will to your fantasies. . . ."[31]

In fact, when God moved her to marry, she would do nothing to give the realm cause for discontent. "I will never in that matter conclude anything that shall be prejudicial to the realm, for the weal, good, and safety whereof I will never shun to spend my life."[32] And if she did not marry, the Commons must not fear, for God would guide her and them in securing an heir who would be a good governor.

For although I be never so careful of your well doings and mind ever so to be, yet may my issue grow out of kind and become perhaps ungracious. And in the end, this shall be for me sufficient, that a marble stone shall declare that a Queen, having reigned such a time, lived and died a virgin.[33]

One may think this word reminding each of his proper place will be sufficient. Not for the Commons! Again, after the queen's narrow escape from death in 1563, they returned with more petitions and received yet another answer.

Addressing the Speaker, the queen remarked, that since the Commons represented the whole realm, she would overcome her bashfulness, forget her lack of wit, and answer their petition. Because the matter of marriage and fixing the succession was so great, she must have grave advice. Since the benefit of the realm and the safety of all were involved, she must defer her answer to some other time. Much thanks were, however, owed to the Commons for their concern over her safety. Though God had chastised her in this illness, she needed not have been further reminded that she was mortal. This she knew.

I know also that I must seek to discharge myself of that great burthen that God hath laid upon me. For of them to whom much is committed much is required. Think not that I, that in other matters have had convenient care of you all, will in this matter, touching the safety of myself and you all, be careless. For I know that this matter toucheth me much nearer than it doth you all, who if the worst happen, can lose but your bodies; but if I take not that convenient care that it behoveth me to have therein, I hazard to lose both body and soul.[34]

Elizabeth reminded the Commons of her responsibility to God and told them that she was concerned about their safety,

as I trust you likewise do not forget that by me you were delivered whilst you were handing on the bough ready to fall into the mud, yea to be drowned in the dung, neither yet [do you forget] the promise which you have here made concerning your duties and due obedience, wherewith, I assure you, I mean to charge you.[35]

While reminding them of their responsibility to her, Elizabeth could assure them that she liked their concern for her welfare as expressed in the petition.

. . . I assure you all that, though after my death you may have many stepdames, yet shall you never have a more natural mother than I mean to be unto you all.[36]

Petition they might, but demand or coerce, never. Children should look to their parent for guidance in serious matters!

To reinforce her answer to the Common's petition, Elizabeth delivered a short speech at the closing of the 1563 Parliament. The skillful monarch never really answered the request in this delightful piece of equivocation. To her, it was important for a prince to keep her word unspotted. So, she would answer them. Some suggested that the queen had a vow against marriage. This was not true. "For though I can think it best for a private woman, yet do I strive with myself to think it not meet for a Prince. And if I can bend my liking to your need, I will not resist such a

---

[31] J. E. Neale, *Elizabeth I and Her Parliaments 1559–1581* (New York, 1958), pp. 48–49. Cited below as Neale I. See also his *Queen Elizabeth I* (Garden City, 1957), chap. III. Neale's rendering of the queen's speeches is the most authoritative and is gratefully followed hereafter.

[32] Neale I, p. 49.
[33] Neale I, p. 49.

[34] Neale I, p. 108.
[35] Neale I, p. 108.
[36] Neale I, p. 109.

mind."[37] She likewise would not rush precipitously to settle the succession. There were many reasons to consider, some of which the Parliament was not aware. "But I hope I shall die in quiet with *nunc dimittis,* which cannot be without I see some glimpse of your following surety after my graved bones."[38] Inscrutable is the Deity, and Elizabeth too! The prince would not be forced against her will; for surely she alone saw all sides of the question.

But youth was incorrigible. In the 1566 Parliament the members were at it again. Succession and marriage, the same old refrain. To forestall any further petitioning, the queen summoned a select delegation of Lords and Commons to hear her views and possibly stay any further proceedings in the matter. Her wrath was full as she lashed out at the indiscreet mouths in the House of Commons who had chosen to make a public spectacle of the matter. These members were not satisfied with showing their Englishry by patriotically stating that their country would perish if the succession was not fixed. No, they had proceeded to entreat the aid of the upper house, ". . . whereby you [the Lords] were seduced, and of simplicity did assent unto it. . . ."[39] Yet, she knew that her Lords had intended no malice nor would have done this if they had sufficiently considered the importance of the matter. Yet, in the House of Lords, the bishops had taken up the cry that her death without issue would be dangerous. She knew this as well as they did. Reaching the peak of her righteous indignation, the queen continued her attack against the offenders:

And so it was easy to be seen *quo oratio tendit.* For those that should be stops and stays of this great good, and [responsible for] avoiding of so many dangers and perils, how evil might they seem to be! And so to aggravate the cause against me! Was I not born in this realm? Where my parents born in any foreign country? Is there any cause I should alienate myself from being careful over this country? Is not my kingdom here? Whom have I oppressed? Whom have I enriched to other's harm? What turmoil have I made in this Commonwealth that I should be suspected to have no regard to the same? How have I governed since my reign? I will be tried by envy itself. I need not use many words, for my deeds do try me.[40]

She well knew that the clamor was over the succession. Although she had already in this session sent word to the House through her privy councillors to cease discussion, this message had not been credited, "although spoken by their Prince." What more could really be said on the subject? "I will never break the word of a prince, spoken in a public place, for my honour's sake," the queen continued. "And therefore I say again, I will marry as soon as I can conveniently. . . . And I hope to have children, otherwise I would never marry."[41] What firmer statement could subjects desire? Indeed they were "a strange order of petitioners, that will make a request and cannot be otherwise ascertained but by their Prince's word, and yet will never believe it when it is spoken."[42] No matter what was said or done, these very persons would not be content, either with the promise or with a future spouse. "Well, there was never so great a treason but might be covered under as fair a pretense."[43]

Turning to the limitation of the succession, the queen was annoyed that in all the discussion nothing had been said of her safety. The only thought had been for their own safety. This was a marvelous state of affairs:

A strange thing that the foot should direct the head in so weighty a cause; which cause hath been so diligently weighed by us, for that it toucheth us more than them. I am sure there were not one of them that ever was a second person, as I have been, and have tasted of the practices against my sister. . . . There were occasions in me at that time. I stood in danger of my life, my sister was so incensed against me: I did differ from her in religion, and I was sought for divers ways. And so shall never be my successor.[44]

This stricture invoking her position and drawing upon her own experience surely indicated the queen's conception of what belonged legitimately to her province and afforded insight into her desire to prevent the mad scramble for place and favor that the fixing of this succession would produce. Plots and counter-plots were not the queen's idea of a healthy commonwealth.

Elizabeth continued that she was not oblivious to the dangers that ensued from limitation of the succession. If her reason did not prevail, she would gladly let the Commons handle the problem. The competitors for office and preference would be so many that "it would be an occasion of a greater charge than a subsidy."[45] Thus far, the queen had spoken of the perils to the realm. But she would put her hearers in mind of her own role in their concerns.

As for my own part, I care not for death; for all men are mortal. And though I be a woman, yet I have as good a courage, answerable to my place, as ever my father had. I am your anointed Queen. I thank God I am endued with such qualities that if I were turned out of the realm in my petticoat, I were able to live in any place in Christendom.[46]

So she hoped they would better understand not only their own peril but hers also. It was not convenient to limit the succession now; nor would it ever be without danger to them and her. But when there was no peril to them, though danger to her would always be present, the queen told the Commons, "I will deal

---

[37] Neale I, p. 127.
[38] Neale I, p. 127.
[39] Neale I, p. 146.
[40] Neale I, p. 147.
[41] Neale I, p. 147.
[42] Neale I, p. 147.
[43] Neale I, p. 148.
[44] Neale I, p. 148.
[45] Neale I, p. 149.
[46] Neale I, p. 149.

therein for your safety, and offer it unto you as your Prince and head without request; for it is monstrous that the feet should direct the head." [47] Of the proper function of each estate, the queen had no doubt. Hers was the initiative in matters touching the crown. Hot heads must beware of casting aspersions on the good intentions and faithfulness of their dread prince.

As the session closed, one could see in the background the succession controversy and the related issue of the liberties of the House to discuss the matter. With these conflicts in mind, it was natural that the queen should desire to set all aright before the members returned home. Elizabeth enjoined her listeners to avoid being misled in their actions. For the succession, it certainly was better that so great a matter have "his original from a zealous Prince's consideration, not from so lip-laboured orations out of such subjects' mouths ... [that] ... have done their lewd endeavour to make all my realm suppose that their care was much, when mine was none at all." [48]

Moving to the crux of her remarks, Elizabeth took up the problem of liberties. She endeavored to show how her commands had been misunderstood and at the same time to establish the proper relationship between prince and Commons:

As to liberties, who is so simple that doubts whether a Prince that is head of all the body may not command the feet not to stray when they would slip? God forbid that your liberty should make my bondage, or that your lawful liberties should anyways have been infringed. No, no, my commandment tended to no whit to that end: lawfulness of which commandment, if I had not more pitied you than blamed you, might easily by good right be showed you.[49]

Nevertheless, the queen did not question their loyalty or devotion to her. Surely, they had been deceived in this matter of liberties. On the other hand, "so I am persuaded you will not beguile the assured joy that ever I took to see my subjects' love to me more staunch than ever I felt the care in myself for myself to be great; which alone hath made my heavy burden light, and a kingdom's care but easy carriage for me." [50] In conclusion, the queen modulated her rebuke to one of sweet understanding for their aims in her behalf:

Let this my discipline stand you in stead of sorer strokes, never to tempt too far a Prince's patience; and let my comfort pluck up your dismayed spirit, and cause you think that, in hope that your following behaviours shall make amends for past actions, you return with your Prince's grace; whose care for you doubt you not to be such as she shall not need a remembrancer for your weal.[51]

Such was the charm that the queen was able to produce. To turn a turbulent session to full advantage required a master. Elizabeth once again maintained a public image in which she appeared as the sweet gentle prince who could be, however, as stern and firm as her noble father, King Henry VIII.

The speech which Elizabeth delivered at the end of the session of the 1576 Parliament renewed one of the queen's favorite themes—the blessings of her reign. The success of the reign was due not to her but to God. One special item struck her as significant, that she had so long been assured of the zeal of her faithful subjects, which had been a special comfort to her.

Can a Prince, that of necessity must discontent a number to delight and please a few (because the greatest part is oft not the best inclined), continue so long time without great offence, much mislike, or common grudge? Or haps it oft that Prince's acts are conceived in so good part, and favourably interpreted? No, no, my Lords. How great my fortune is in this respect, I were ingrate if I should not acknowledge. And as for those rare and special benefits which many years have followed and accompanied me with happy reign, I attribute them to God alone, the Prince of rule, and account myself no better than his handmaid: rather brought up in a school to abide the ferula, than traded in a kingdom to support the sceptre.[52]

Throughout her reign, she had not been guided by mere policy and wordly wisdom, as her attitude on religion and marriage testified. Rather she had given up these approaches to seek Truth. She had trusted in God and would continue to do so. If her hearers considered the plight of neighboring countries—whose maladies she would not attribute to their princes—they could well appreciate the blessings of her reign. She would also have them remember that it was easier for private persons to criticize than mend a prince's state. Therefore, both they and she must pray to God for guidance and work with the best of their abilities to further the commonweal.[53] Elizabeth was not indifferent to their petition that she marry. Yet, they knew that she had no personal desire to marry. Nevertheless, she would not let her personal predilections interfere with the good of their estate. Still, in all these grave matters, "let good heed be taken that, in reaching too far after future good, you peril not the present and begin to quarrel, and fall by dispute together by the ears, before it be decided who shall wear my crown." [54] In conclusion, she admonished them to understand that before she died, she hoped God would grant her "some good way for your full safety." Could they, dared they hope for more? Once again, Elizabeth captured her hearers' hearts by her gentleness and willingness to share with them the thought that all were engaged in a common task, one that she did not take lightly.

Amid the anxiety of insuring the queen's safety that took up so much time in the Parliament of 1584–1585 and the desire to reform abuses in religion, the queen's speech at the closing of Parliament once more reflected

---

[47] Neale I, p. 150.
[48] Neale I, p. 174.
[49] Neale I, p. 175.
[50] Neale I, p. 175.
[51] Neale I, p. 176.

[52] Neale I, p. 365.
[53] Neale I, pp. 365–366.
[54] Neale I, p. 367.

her radiant and beneficent nature. This Parliament had passed the "Act for the Surety of the Queen's Person" that has linked many to the task of preserving the sovereign's life. With this show of loyalty from her people, Elizabeth could well state:

No Prince herein, I confess, can be surer tied or faster bound than I am with the link of your good will; and can for that but yield a heart and head to seek for ever all your best.

The refrain was so familiar, but the theme had shifted from marriage to religion:

Yet one matter toucheth me so near, as I may not overskip: religion, the ground on which all other matters ought to take root, and, being corrupted, may mar all the tree; and that there be some faultfinders with the order of the clergy, which so may make a slander of myself and the Church, whose overruler God hath made me, whose negligence cannot be excused if any schisms or errors heretical were suffered.[55]

She was determined that the bishops should redress all of these grievances or answer to her for their neglect. The queen had never been indifferent, as some had said, to religion. Even now, she was hourly in peril for it. So, if she was not convinced "that mine were the true way of God's will, God forbid I should live to prescribe it to you."[56] Too many tried to analyze the scriptures as lawyers examined human testaments. The queen would not suffer this to continue. Neither papists nor Puritans would be permitted to upset the religious settlement.

And of the latter, I must pronounce them dangerous to a kingly rule: to have every man, accordng to his own censure, to make a doom of the validity and privity of his Prince's government, with a common veil and cover of God's word, whose followers must not be judged but by private man's exposition. God defend you from such a ruler that so evil will guide you.[57]

There could be no doubt that Elizabeth felt that the prince was responsible for the maintenance of true religion. As she had indicated before, the prince could not suffer any group to upset the social order that was ultimately founded upon religion. Her strictures against Puritanism showed her insight into the logic of their system. Their program would upset the whole microcosm. If Elizabeth's view was rigorously pressed, one would find no room for toleration. The official mystique required one Prince, one Commonwealth, one Faith.

Mary queen of Scots dominated the deliberations of the Parliament of 1586–1587. The queen of Scots was considered a menace to the safety of Elizabeth and the realm. It was the feeling of the Parliament that one life must be sacrificed to save another. A committee of both Houses twice asked the queen to take action against Mary, and twice Elizabeth asked them to accept her "answer-answerless." In these speeches, so filled with the emotion of a troubled heart, the queen fervently hoped that her subjects might in some way remove the cup from her and understand why she could not resolve the problem. Elizabeth desired above all else to preserve both her own life and Mary's. What is significant for our purposes is Elizabeth's acute awareness of the function of a prince and the qualities that a prince must have. Her argument was that having tried to follow her duty, she was now confronted with a situation that virtually prevented her from being a good prince.

Regardless of what previous actions had been taken against Mary, or might be suggested by others, Elizabeth must decide the Scottish queen's fate. She alone must bear the responsibility. As she reminded her audience:

... we Princes, I tell you, are set on stages, in the sight and view of all the world duly observed. The eyes of many behold our actions; a spot is soon spied in our garments, a blemish quickly noted in our doings. It behooveth us, therefore, to be careful that our proceedings be just and honourable.[58]

Hence, Elizabeth must seek to "determine that which shall serve to the establishment of His Church, preservation of your estates, and prosperity of this Commonwealth under my charge."[59] So, in her second address, she continued to emphasize the qualities she had so long practiced: "... I, who have in my time pardoned so many rebels, winked at so many treasons, and either not produced them or altogether slipped them over with silence, should not be forced to this proceeding, against such a person."[60] The thought of taking a royal life was not a pleasant one for a clement prince.

The queen was grateful for her subjects' concern for her welfare. Yet, her Commons must understand her deep feelings in this matter. If they appreciated this fact, they would understand why she could not proceed with the business. The following revealed much of the queen's inner feelings about her role as prince:

I was not simply trained up, nor in my youth spent my time altogether idly; and yet, when I came to the crown, then entered I first into the school of experience, bethinking myself of those things that best fitted a king—justice, temper, magnanimity, judgment. As for the latter two, I will not boast. But for the two first, this may I truly say: among my subjects I never knew a difference of person, where right was one; nor never to my knowledge preferred for favour what I thought not fit for worth; nor bent mine ears to credit a tale that first was told me; nor was so rash to corrupt my judgment with my censure, ere I heard the cause. I will not say but many reports might fortune be brought me by such as must hear the matter, whose partiality might mar the right; for we Princes cannot hear all causes ourselves. But this dare I boldly affirm: my verdict went with the truth of my knowledge.[61]

---

[55] J. E. Neale, *Elizabeth I and Her Parliaments 1584–1601* (New York, 1958), p. 99. Cited below as Neale II.
[56] Neale II, p. 100.
[57] Neale II, p. 100.
[58] Neale II, p. 119.
[59] Neale II, p. 120.
[60] Neale II, p. 127.
[61] Neale II, p. 128.

Against a background of an attempted Spanish invasion, the Parliament of 1593 voted a generous subsidy. In her speech at the close of the session, Elizabeth thanked them for what they had done for her and the commonwealth. All her own efforts and "the travail of my thoughts chiefly tendeth to God's service and the government of you, to live in a flourishing and happy estate." [62] They had had wiser princes than Elizabeth, but "none whose love and care can be greater or whose desire can be more to fathom deeper for prevention of danger to come, or resisting of dangers if attempted towards you, shall ever be found to exceed myself. In love, I say, towards you, and care over you." [63] Though there was talk of danger once more, the queen did not fear, for God was on her side because her cause was just. One thing more she would have them do. As the enemy feared their valor, she would have them return to their homes to promote confidence in the people and attend to any necessary preparations for an invasion.[64]

Brief though the speech was, it contained two insights of worth. First, the queen desired once again to impress on her hearers that their welfare was uppermost in her mind. Second, Elizabeth's injunction to the Parliament to spread confidence among her people indicated that she fully realized the importance of presenting her views to the Parliament. Her speeches created in the minds of her hearers an image that she wished conveyed to all quarters of the realm. This short speech was a prologue to two final speeches of the reign, in which the queen rendered to the people her last solemn account of her stewardship.

The Parliament of 1601 was the last occasion for the actress to perform. In two speeches, one to the Commons, the other at the close of the session, Elizabeth rendered her eloquent valedictory. The occasion for her "Golden Speech" to the Commons was the problem of monopolies and its happy solution. The queen graciously thanked the Speaker who had expressed the gratitude of the whole House for her redress of their grievance.

I do assure you that there is no prince that loves his subjects better, or whose love can countervail our love. There is no jewel, be it of never so rich a price, which I set before this jewel: I mean your love. For I do esteem it more than any treasure or riches; for that we know how to prize, but love and thanks I count unvaluable. And, though God hath raised me high, yet this I count the glory of my crown, that I have reigned with your loves. This makes me that I do not so much rejoice that God hath made me to be a Queen, as to be a Queen over so thankful a people.[65]

She did not desire to live longer than she could be of service to them. It was Elizabeth's hope that as she, under God, had delivered them in the past from danger and oppression, so she might still be able to do.

Considering her relation to her subjects, "of myself I must say this: I never was any greedy, scraping grasper, nor a strait, fast-holding Prince, nor yet a waster." All that had been given her by her people she had used for their advancement. "Yea, mine own properties I account yours, to be expended for your good; and your eyes shall see the bestowing of all for your good." [66]

On the subject of monopolies the queen wished all to know that her intentions were always to do the proper thing. Therefore, she was most thankful that her faithful Commons had called her attention to the abuse of her trust and authority by others. "That my grants should be grievous to my people and oppressions privileged under colour of our patents, our kingly dignity shall not suffer it." [67] The culprits would not go unpunished. For, "I have even used to set the Last-Judgment Day before mine eyes, and so to rule as I shall be judged to answer before a higher Judge, to whose judgment seat I do appeal, that never thought good." [68] Many felt that it was glorious to be a king. Yet, Elizabeth would have all know that, "to be a King and wear a crown is a thing more glorious to them that see it, than it is pleasant to them that bear it." [69] All her efforts had been to promote God's truth and do his will.

One major conclusion Elizabeth wanted them to grasp:

though you have had and may have many princes more mighty and wise sitting in this seat, yet you never had nor shall have any that will be more careful and loving.[70]

In her speech at the closing of the session, the queen surveyed the whole course of her foreign and domestic policies. She reminded all that she had ever tried to act justly and uprightly in all her dealings. Every effort had been made to conserve her people's love. All the subsidies and her own revenues had been used to defend and prosper her country. The queen had been content "to be a taper of true virgin wax, to waste myself and spend my life that I might give light and comfort to those that live under me." [71]

In foreign affairs, Elizabeth recounted all her endeavors with foreign princes, particularly the Spanish king, to promote the peace and well-being of all peoples. She had never looked for war, though she had received it in return for her own good offices. This account of her policy she rendered "that you may perceive how free your Queen is from any cause of these attempts that have been made on her, unless to save her people or defend her state be censured. This testimony I would have you carry hence for the world to know: that your Sovereign is more careful of your conservation than of

---

[62] Neale II, p. 321.
[63] Neale II, p. 322.
[64] Neale II, p. 322.
[65] Neale II, p. 388.
[66] Neale II, p. 389.
[67] Neale II, p. 390.
[68] Neale II, p. 390.
[69] Neale II, p. 391.
[70] Neale II, p. 391.
[71] Neale II, p. 428.

herself, and will daily crave of God, that they that wish you best may never wish in vain." [72] So the actress uttered her last public speech to the realm.

In her speeches Elizabeth presented a portrait of the prince that incorporated many of the features presented by the statesmen. The queen showed that the ruler was bound by the law of God and, therefore, must constantly think of the well-being of her subjects. For someday the ruler must render to God an account of her stewardship. As the head of the state, the prince had the ultimate responsibility for the conduct of public policy and for the proper conduct of her lesser officials.

Impelled by this sense of responsibility, the prince looked after the moral and material welfare of her subjects. Thus, the queen gave unstintingly of her own talents and resources to improve and protect the commonwealth. To carry out these functions, the sovereign must exercise the royal prerogative without the interference of misguided souls—particularly members of the House of Commons. While the prince was clement and just, one must not infer that these qualities were a sign of weakness. Therefore, subjects should not meddle in high matters of state that were within the scope of the prerogative. Such areas reserved for the crown were religion and the conduct of foreign affairs. Another area in which the queen was absolute was her private life. The prince could not be forced against her will to marry. Finally, the queen had the duty to inform her subjects of the state of the commonwealth, to ask their assistance in remedying abuses, and to secure this financial support. Thus, Elizabeth maintained that each estate must respect the rights and privileges of the others. The prince must be given honor and reverence. In return, she would give her life for the benefit of her people.

4.

The portrait of the prince that emerges from the preceding discussion is one that is accepted by prince and people. The first major point is that the prince is subject to law. This law is of two types. In one instance, the prince is limited by the customary law of the land—the common law. On the other side, the ruler is subject to the law of nature, which is the moral structure of the universe. Thus, in both these instances, the prince is not an unlimited ruler, at least theoretically.

In a constitutional sense, the monarch is not absolute. Thus, he is not the source of law or its final arbiter. Only the King-in-Parliament is the absolute judge. Beyond this High Court of Parliament, there is no appeal. The prince cannot change the customary or positive law without the consent of all estates of the kingdom. Conversely, the Lords and Commons cannot alter the law without the prince's consent. While the ruler is not in a legal sense absolute, he does exercise the royal prerogative. By this prerogative, the prince exercises complete control of the coinage, the conduct of foreign affairs, the appointment and removal of lesser officials, the dispensing and pardoning powers, and the emergency war power. In these areas, there is little practical check on the monarch's power.

From this broad picture of the nature of royal authority, certain important corollaries follow. First, the prince has the duty to suppress rebellion and protect the realm from foreign invasion. The ruler also has the right to administer justice and take measures to promote the general welfare. Sir Thomas Smith, Lord Burghley, and the queen equally maintained these points and avoided one crucial item. None of the writers critically examined the doctrine of the right of the subject openly and actively to resist authority. Smith counseled that it was inadvisable to upset the existing order of the commonwealth. The queen and Lord Burghley simply asserted the obligation of the prince to maintain order.

The rights of the prince in matters of religion receive uneven treatment by the writers considered, in the preceding analysis. Smith carefully avoided the issue in his work. Burghley suggested that the monarch did not desire to pry into the private beliefs of her subjects and that the prince only insisted upon external conformity to the ecclesiastical order established by law. Burghley further argued that the cloak of religion might not be used to cover treasonable acts. Rebellion could not be palmed off as religious conviction.

However, the views of Sir Thomas Wilson and the speeches of the queen presented another view of religion. In this view, the prince had a definite responsibility for the spiritual well-being of the subjects. As Sir Thomas argued, the commonwealth was essentially a moral instrument. Its function was to carry out the will of God in human affairs. Therefore, the prince, as its head, must assume the primary responsibility in spiritual matters, and the queen's speeches suggested that Elizabeth, at least publicly, maintained the same sense of responsibility.

Throughout the entire analysis one finds that the prince must be wise, just, clement, understanding, diligent, and merciful. In short, the virtues of the prince must reflect Christian principles of conduct. For even the prince must finally render an account of her work to God.

In the picture of the prince, one theme is constantly repeated. The prince is limited legally and morally by the customs of the realm and the order of nature. Whether in Smith's idea of a commonwealth formed by free men for a common purpose, in Wilson's idea that the minister and the magistrate should work more closely together, or in the queen's rejection of any idea of sacerdotal power in her title of "Supreme Governour," the concept of order and degree are constantly reiterated. This ideal of order and degree is essentially moral in nature. For the commonwealth and its sev-

---
[72] Neale II, p. 431.

eral estates are instruments to do the will of God. While one may be impressed with the lofty concept of the prince that is presented by the highest temporal authorities of Elizabethan England, one dares not overlook the crucial ingredient. The queen herself suggests that the royal mystique works because the prince rules with the love of her people. In the final analysis the practical, not the theoretical principles, make the commonwealth function.

IV. OUR DREAD SOVEREIGN LADY

The theories of kingship developed by churchmen and statesmen attained ultimate validation in the crucible of the courts of law. The royal courts, therefore, were the most effective and formidable ones in applying the theories of kingship to the practicalities of daily life. The vast body of statutory and case law which circumscribed the civil and criminal activities of Elizabethans afforded many examples in which the sovereign and the subject were arrayed against each other as adversaries and from which emerged certain principles of legal conduct which illumined the nature of kingship. No part of the law was more fruitful in this respect than the criminal law which enumerated and defined the most heinous offenses against individuals and the commonwealth.

While it has been suggested that all crimes, whether misdemeanors, felonies, or treasons, constituted breaches against the king's peace or threatened the well-being of society, none were deemed more serious than those which challenged the very existence of the commonwealth personified and symbolized in the prince. Within the criminal law, such manifestations of acute anti-social behavior were treated under the classification of treason.[1] In Elizabethan jurisprudence, the most serious type of this classification was high treason. It is the purpose of this chapter, therefore, to examine the concept of high treason as an expression of the deepest held convictions about the doctrine of the prince set forth in the law.

The enacted law and the case law were the two major divisions of the concept of treason, and their interpretation and application were the function of the appropriate courts. In general, the High Court of Parliament, the court of the Lord High Steward of England, and the court of Queen's Bench resolved matters of high treason in accordance with rules of procedure and evidence received from the common law or prescribed by the enacted law.[2] Certainly, the use of special commissions of oyer and terminer in the trials of commoners and the frequent gaps between the theoretical and actual adherence to rules of procedure and evidence suggested in the actual cases provide an important caution to the above generalizations. Given the nature of the law, therefore, this chapter will examine first the statutory formulations of treason which were in force at various times during the reign of Elizabeth. Second, an examination of the relevant case law will follow. In both instances, a representative approach will be taken. From this study, certain conclusions will emerge about the nature of kingship as it was mirrored in the collective judgment of those responsible for the preservation of society.

1.

The basis of the Elizabethan concept of treason rested upon the definitive statement of Parliament in the statute of 1352. Declaratory in nature, the law presented the major areas of treasonable offenses. Acting in any of the following ways, one was guilty of high treason: first, when a man compassed or imagined the death of the king, his queen, their eldest son and heir; second, if a man violated the king's companion, or violated the eldest unmarried daughter of the king, or if he violated the wife of the eldest son and heir of the king; third, if a man levied war against the king in his realm, or if he were adherent to the king's enemies in his realm, giving aid and comfort to them in the realm or elsewhere, and thereof were provably attainted of open deed by people of their condition. Fourth, if a man counterfeited the king's great seal or privy seal, or his money; fifth, if a man brought false money into the realm counterfeit to the money of England knowing the money to be false, to merchandize or make payment, in deceit of the king and his people; and sixth, if a man slew the chancellor, treasurer, justices of one bench or the other, justices in eyre, or justices of assize, and all other justices assigned to hear and determine, being in their places doing their offices. Finally, the statute stated:

Because other like cases of treason may happen in time to come, which cannot be thought of nor declared at present, it is accorded, that if any other cause supposed to be treason, which is not above specified, doth happen before any judge, the judge shall tarry without going to judgment of the treason, till the cause be showed and declared before the king and his parliament, whether it ought to be judged treason or other felony.[3]

The statute of Edward III contributed four major ideas to the concept of treason. It contained the idea of treachery, that of a breach of the feudal bond, the concept of duty to the king transcending duty to a feudal lord, and a notion of *laesa majestas* derived from Roman law. This last idea applied to the falsification

---

[1] For classical legal discussions of the nature of high treason see 3 *Co. Inst.* 1–9; and 4 *Bl Comm.* 74–92. Treason as discussed here refers to high treason unless otherwise noted in the chapter.

[2] Sir William Holdsworth, *A History of English Law* (London, 1966), 4: pp. 492–500; and Sir James F. Stephen, *A History of the Criminal Law of England* (London, 1883) 1: chap. XI, esp. pp. 330–331; and 2: chap. XXIII. See also Samuel Rezneck, "History of the Parliamentary Declaration of Treason," *Law Quart. Rev.* 181 (1930): pp. 80–102.

[3] 25 Edward III, St. 5, c. 2. See also Holdsworth, 2: pp. 449–451; and 3: pp. 287–293.

of Caesar's image, a form of sacrilege. The law also safeguarded the subject from capricious charges of treason without sacrificing the safety of the prince and those most closely associated with his well-being and proper functioning.[4] The precision and clarity of these personalized definitions of treason, however, did not always meet the exigencies of later ages, including those of the sixteenth century. The king of the statute of 1352 was not the one of the case of the Duchy of Lancaster. The law's concepts offered little support for those of the royal supremacy in ecclesiastical causes and of the succession to the throne, often subsumed in the the idea of the crown imperial.[5] To give these new ideas force, the Tudors resorted to new statutory definitions of treason which often lapsed with the death of a particular sovereign. During the reign of Elizabeth, this practice continued in order to make the concept of treason conform to the needs of state policy. This legislation extended and elaborated definitions contained in the statute of Edward III, developed the ideas inherited from the earlier Tudors, and sought to protect the queen from new perils and exalt her office. The Elizabethan definitions of treason, moreover, fell into three major categories: the first comprehended matters of religion, the second included matters affecting the safety of the queen and the surety of the succession, and the third encompassed matters pertaining to the national security and prosperity.

The first Elizabethan statute which extended the definitions of treason in the religious sphere was the act of supremacy, 1 Elizabeth c. 1.[6] While the act asserted the supremacy of the imperial crown in causes ecclesiastical, it also indicated what actions in derogation of this authority constituted treason upon a third conviction. If any person by writing, printing, teaching, or preaching advisedly, maliciously, or directly affirmed, set forth, or defended the ecclesiastical or spiritual jurisdiction of any foreign prince, prelate, or potentate within the realm, he was guilty of treason. Likewise, if a person put into use or executed anything which asserted such claims to jurisdiction, he committed a treason. Two witnesses were required to declare such allegations and were required to so testify at the arraignment if the accused so required. Peers were to be tried by peers.

"An Act for the assurance of the Queens Majesty's Royal power over all Estates and subjects within her Highness's Dominions," 5 Elizabeth c. 1, built upon the act of supremacy. The penalties of high treason were incurred if a person upon a second conviction had by writing, printing, ciphering, preaching, or teaching asserted or defended knowingly the authority of the Roman bishops within Elizabeth's dominions. A person who attributed such power to Rome, together with those who purposefully aided him, if convicted a second time, incurred similar penalties. Refusal to take the oath of supremacy when offered a second time constituted treason without corruption in blood. To bolster this law, the 1571 Parliament enacted one which prohibited the importation and execution of papal bulls and instruments in England, 13 Elizabeth c. 2.[7]

This law denounced those who sought to subvert the established religion under guise of papal promises of absolution, condemned those who preyed upon the weak, simple, and ignorant to forsake their allegiance to God and the queen, and noted that such efforts had produced "wycked and unnatural Rebellyon." The commission of the following offenses, therefore, constituted treason. First, the use of papal bulls and other instruments within the realm was included. The second definition covered those who acted under such papal documents to reconcile people to Rome by open deed or other methods of communication. The third provision included those who willingly accepted absolution or accepted reconciliation with Rome. Those who obtained papal bulls and instruments "contayning any Thinge Matter or Cause whatsoever" fell under a fourth class. Finally, the publication or use of other ways of implementing papal bulls was defined as treason. Accessories to the fact of such actions were regarded as principals in the law. "An Act to retain the Queen's Majesty's Subjects in their due Obedience," 23 Elizabeth c. 1, reaffirmed the penalties against those who had or pretended to have power to or did absolve persuade or withdraw any subject from his natural obedience to Elizabeth. Moreover, to withdraw a subject "for that intent" from the established religion to "The Romyshe Religion" or induce him to promise obedience to Rome or any other prince who claimed authority within the realm was defined as treason. A person who voluntarily submitted to such pretended authority was also defined as a traitor. The capstone of this particular class of laws was that against Jesuits and seminary priests, 27 Elizabeth c. 2. Proclaiming that these persons sought to destroy Elizabeth, the law banished them from the realm with a specified period of time. If such priests, deacons, or other religious persons remained in England or entered it after this date, that act constituted a treasonable offense. The statute also required Englishmen studying abroad in Jesuit colleges or Catholic seminaries to return home as directed by the crown. Failure to return within a fixed time period and failure to take the oath of supremacy upon return were defined also as treasons.

These laws presented a concept of the prince which was more abstract and metaphysical than that portrayed

---

[4] Holdsworth, 3: pp. 289–290.

[5] William Huse Dunham, Jr., "The Crown Imperial," *Parliamentary Affairs* 6 (1952): pp. 199–206.

[6] The acts cited in this part are from *Statutes of the Realm* (London, repr. ed., 1963) 4: 1 and 2.

[7] J. E. Neale, *Elizabeth I and Her Parliaments 1559–1581* (New York, 1958), pp. 225–234.

in the 1352 statute. The safety of the prince was now linked to the security of the established religion. Acts and persons that threatened this safety were to be punished and removed from the commonwealth. For, these laws sought to protect both the natural body and the politic body of the sovereign. In a sense, the Roman legal idea of desecrating the image of the prince embedded in the law of Edward III to cover counterfeiting now was extended to include the defacing of the religious image of the prince. Sacrilege had become a species of treason comprehending the established religion. In a curious way, the Roman idea of the sanctity of the gods and of Caesar had come to fruition in the Elizabethan idea of the sacredness of the prince and her religion.[8]

The second major group of statutes was designed to protect the safety of the queen and the security of the succession. These laws continued, therefore, to develop the concept of the king's two bodies symbolized in the crown imperial. In 1 Elizabeth c. 5, definitions of treason were set forth which applied to the question of the succession, upon a second conviction. Maliciously and advisedly to compass and imagine to deprive the queen or the heirs of her body from the style, dignity, and kingly name of the crown imperial of the realm and dominions annexed to it constituted the first definition. Second, to destroy the prince or her issue, or to levy war against her or them within the realm and the dominions, or to depose her or her issue from the crown were additional classes of treason. To expound advisedly and maliciously such compassings and imaginings by preaching, express words, or sayings formed yet a third form of offense. The malicious and advised statement, publication, or declaration that the queen was not or ought not to have been the legitimate sovereign of the realm, or that her issue ought not to be rulers after her death, or that other than her issue should rule of right as long as her own descendents lived were clear acts of treason.

This act also provided definitions of treason which were connected to the legitimacy of Elizabeth's title. For example, to assert directly and maliciously by writing, printing, or other overt act that Elizabeth ought not have the kingly name of the realm, or that someone else should have it in her place, or that Elizabeth ought not to be or was not rightfully queen during her life formed another set of offenses. Moreover, to assert in similar ways and with similar motives that the queen's issue ought not to enjoy of right the imperial crown, or that someone other than her issue ought to have the right to the crown was another treason. Significantly, the law provided that prosecutions for treason by words had to occur within six months after the alleged utterance, and required the testimony of two witnesses at the time of indictment and arraignment unless one freely confessed the violation.

An even more comprehensive treasons act emerged in 13 Elizabeth c. 1. This law covered the personal safety of the monarch, the problem of the succession and potential claimants, and then the rule of law in such matters. The first section of the act defined treason first to cover those who within or without the realm compassed, imagined, or intended the death and destruction or any such action that tended to the harm of the queen, or those who deposed or deprived Elizabeth of the crown of the realm and of the dominions, or those who levied war against her within or without the realm. The section also provided that those who sought foreign aid to invade England, Ireland, or the other dominions, or those who uttered or declared in any manner such compassings and intentions, or those who declared, held, or affirmed that Elizabeth was not and ought not to be the sovereign of all the territories claimed by her, or held that someone else should rule these realms during the queen's life, or who affirmed by any means that Elizabeth was a heretic, schismatic, tyrant, infidel, or usurper of the crown were traitors.

Another section of this statute provided that those who held or championed the claims of persons other than Elizabeth to be rulers contrary to royal proclamation and those who asserted such claims in contradiction to royal declarations fell under the definition of high treason. The final set of definitions pertained to the determination of a lawful succession. Those who denied that the common law as altered by Parliament ought not to determine the succession, or who denied that Elizabeth and Parliament could not make laws to fix effectively the succession were traitors. Finally, to deny the binding character of parliamentary legislation regulating the succession or asserting the queen's right to the crown completed the legal definitions. In short, these declarations of treason vastly expanded those of the statute of Edward III. Combined with 1 Elizabeth c. 5, these statements had integrated the personal safety of the prince into that of the dynasty. The prince lived on in her issue, and thus, the future prince was protected in the present one. It was a vivid confirmation of the idea that the king never dies.

Four statutes were enacted which reflected the traditional concerns of the 1352 law and also mirrored the newer concepts. The idea that it was treasonable to counterfeit the royal coinage was augmented by two acts, 5 Elizabeth c. 1, and 18 Elizabeth c. 1. Both laws made it an offense to mutilate in any manner or to diminish the size and quality of authorized domestic and foreign monies. Clipping, filing, lightening, or scaling down coins constituted treason. It was a logical extension of the older prohibition against counterfeiting and in itself offered no novel conceptual approach to kingship. In the statute of 14 Elizabeth c. 1, the concept of treason was extended to include offenses that deliberately and rebelliously deprived the sovereign of her castles and other fortifications, or those which destroyed

---

[8] Holdsworth, 2: pp. 289–290.

her ships or detained them and other munitions. Likewise, by 14 Elizabeth c. 2, it was a treasonable offense to conspire to set free from prison any person which had been convicted of treason. These four laws, therefore, refined older ideas to meet new conditions. In themselves, they were not daring or exceptionally innovative. However, when placed in the conceptual framework that motived the other Elizabethan statutes, they further emphasized the idea that the protection of the prince from personal harm or incapacity no longer constituted the core of treason expressed in the enacted law.

In the parliamentary definitions of treason, the concept of the prince emerged as a complex one. She was more than a mere person who needed protection against disaffected individuals. She was also a metaphysical reality who needed protection against other abstract realities that threatened her. The extension of treason to include matters of religion, the succession, and even the estate of the realm illustrated that the prince was no longer seen as a mere human being. She was present in the established church, she was embodied in the succession, and she was ever present in her fortresses and ships of the line. There was a quality of ubiquity in the prince that did not appear in the law of Edward III. Certainly, her royal person was well protected in the enacted law, but now also were her various images, like Caesar's, shrouded in sacredness to defend her against all enemies, earthly and ghostly.

2.

The case law had the difficult task of the reconciliation of formal definitions of treason and complex modes of actual behavior. Neat classification on strictly logical grounds was not, therefore, its strong quality. Yet the treasons which concerned it might be generally grouped in five classes. First were offenses affecting religion, second were those related to allegiance, third were offenses affecting the personal safety of the prince, fourth were crimes connected to the general welfare, and fifth were items concerned with due process. Representative examples of these groups which defined the princely doctrine must now be examined.

One of the first judicial tasks concerned with the royal supremacy was to establish applicability of statutory prohibitions on supporting papal authority, 5 Elizabeth c. 1.[9] The judges decided that, if a man imported books which attacked the established religion and disseminated them, he came within the law's compass. Those who read such works and in conference with others approved the contents were also in violation of the law. Individuals who heard contents of such books and approved or who secretly conveyed such material to others in order to enlist more support fell afoul of the law. Moreover, the clandestine publication of these works within the realm and their distribution under the guise of foreign imports constituted violations. A second conviction for this type of act constituted high treason, according to the statute. Thus, the justices of all the benches clearly formulated definitions subsidiary to and operative within a legislative act. Yet, such precautions did not always deter committed souls.

In August, 1570, one John Felton was indicted for publishing the papal bull of excommunication. In May of that year, he had affixed the bull on the door of the bishop of London's palace. Accordingly, the indictment charged him with compassing and imagining the disinheritance, death, and destruction of Elizabeth and with levying war against her. He was also accused of affirming the correctness of the papal charges against his sovereign. The crucial point in the case was the linking of the common law idea of treachery against the prince with that of a denial of the royal supremacy and dignity embodied in statutes of the reign.[10] The idea that a rejection of royal ecclesiastical power constituted an intent to destroy the queen reached a most complete explication in the trials of Edmund Campion and his fellow Jesuits in 1581 and of the earl of Arundel in 1589.[11]

Campion and his friends were accused of conspiring to kill Elizabeth, overthrow the established religion, and subvert the state. The case for the crown sought to establish that the accussed were part of a papal conspiracy against Elizabeth and that these men had willingly and knowingly carried on treasonable activities inside and outside the realm. Under the guise of religious activities, these men had sought to assist the pope through subversion of the crown. One of the key arguments advanced by the crown lawyers was that the oaths of fealty taken by Jesuits to the pope contravened the laws of England. Campion denied these allegations, asserting that he and his friends were being persecuted for their religious beliefs. Sir John Popham, the attorney general, retorted, however, that their religion "might be any cloak or colour of such Treasons."[12] Campion steadfastly denied that he and the others repudiated Elizabeth as their lawful sovereign. Yet, his efforts to separate temporal from religious fealty did not convince the jury. In 1589 Philip, earl of Arundel was convicted of high treason for committing offenses similar to those of the Jesuits. He was accused of harboring Jesuits contrary to law, of being treasonably reconciled to the Church of Rome, of offering assistance to Cardinal Allen, and of offering prayers

---

[9] Dyer, *Reports* (Dublin, 1794), 282a.

[10] P.R.O., *Inventory and Calendar... Baga de secretis. Deputy Keeper's Reports,* IV, app. II, no. 7, pp 265-267. Cited hereafter as *Baga de secretis.*

[11] *R. v. Campion et al.,* 1 State Trials 1049-1071; *R. v. Arundel, Baga de secretis,* pp. 279-281. See also Black, *Reign of Elizabeth,* pp. 179-188; Thomas H. Clancy, S. J., *Papist Pamphleteers* (Chicago, 1964), for a discussion of the Catholic response to Elizabethan policies; and H. R. Trevor-Roper, *Historical Essays* (New York, 1957), pp. 113-118 for a criticism of the Jesuits and their subsequent apologists.

[12] 1 St. Tr. 1056.

for the success of the Spanish Armada.[13] Both cases indicated the equation of religious actions with treasonable ones. They also illustrated that acts to promote a religion contrary to the established one tended to the harm and death of the prince. The cases of Sir John Perrott, lord deputy of Ireland, and of Patrick O'Cullon further employed this approach to defining unacceptable behavior.[14] Religious belief and political action were hardly distinguishable in the case law.

The religious quality of treason established in the preceding cases raised a fundamental question about the nature of allegiance which existed between prince and subject. In the proceedings against Dr. John Story in 1571, this problem was resolved.[15] Accused of conspiring and imagining the queen's death and her deposition as well as of aiding and comforting rebels and plotting an invasion, Story allegedly carried on these acts beyond the seas. The judges maintained that conspiring beyond the seas to invade the realm was intended to place the sovereign in great peril or to destroy her, and, hence, were acts of treason. The justices, therefore, maintained that Story could be tried for these offenses according to the statute 35 Henry VIII c. 2, which provided for such contingencies. Although acknowledging he was a natural born Englishman, Story argued that he had since become a liegeman of Philip of Spain, and, therefore, denied the jurisdiction of English courts and refused to plead to the indictment.[16] Significantly, the judges held that he was subject to the laws of the realm and to the queen. Moreover, because he refused to plead, they proceeded to judgment invoking the principle that standing mute to a treason indictment was equivalent to a plea of guilty. In this case, therefore, the justices clearly established that a subject could not unilaterally break his bond of allegiance to his prince. The subject could not disown his native land nor abjure its head. The judges further re-affirmed the essential concept of treason that it assumed a trusting faithful relationship between prince and subject as normative. Acts to the contrary, as were Story's acts, were heinous, perfidious, and unnatural behavior towards kith and kin embodied in the sovereign, even when committed out of her immediate jurisdiction.[17]

That birth, blood, and personal ties of mutual fidelity bound prince and people was asserted again by the judges later in the reign. A question raised by the chancellor of Ireland to those learned in the law posed it thus: "can a peer of Ireland who leads a rebellion against Elizabeth be tried for his crimes in England?"[18] The reply indicated that he would have to be tried in that kingdom because he was first a subject of Ireland.

The decisions in both instances emphasized that first the subject was personally bound to the sovereign and could not renounce this bond. Second, this intimate personal relationship was mediated through relationships and institutions of often unique and different cultural patterns. An Irish peer was bound to Elizabeth through the medium of that distinctive kingdom of Ireland; likewise, Story was bound through the English realm to Elizabeth. In both cases, the subject could not escape his obligations wherever he happened to be at a given moment. In a real social and legal sense, therefore, the prince embodied the nation and its cultural patterns, and mediated its benefits and rebukes to others. In point of nationality expressed as allegiance, the prince was a mixed person.

Actions which were intended to harm or destroy the sovereign formed the bulk of cases which constituted the third group. While most of the alleged actions involved attempts directly or indirectly to harm the queen, some of them could still be recognized as efforts to harm the metaphysical body of the ruler suggested above. Significantly, however, the latter types of actions were wherever possible subsumed under definitions originally set forth in the treasons statute of Edward III.

At the beginning of the reign, four persons, Thomas Lord Wentworth, Edward Grimston, Sir Ralph Chamberlain, and John Harleston, were indicted for giving aid and comfort to the queen's enemies for their respective roles in the loss of Calais under Mary Tudor. By "secret covin and assent" they conspired with the French king to facilitate enemy occupation of English possessions and had adhered to the French king.[19] Evidence was adduced to support these accusations, but in the instances of Wentworth and Grimston, the senior officials, the charges were not sustained. In the case of Arthur Poole and others, the accusations centered on their conspiracy to depose Elizabeth, "effect her death and total destruction," and place Mary Queen of Scots on the throne.[20] Some of the conspirators, the charges ran, had "practised various incantations and conjurations of evil spirits in working their said affairs; and inquired of an evil spirit how to carry their treasons into effect."[21] Interestingly, the major accusations fell within traditional definitions, though the solicitation of supernatural aid seemed a novel interpretation of adhering to the prince's enemies. These cases set forth the general lines of development in the cases commencing with that of the duke of Norfolk in 1571 and ending with that of the earl of Essex in 1601.

While traditional concepts tended to dominate these trials, the question of the relationship of the true religion to royal safety also emerged, and its solution was accomplished through these cases. For example, the trials of

---

[13] *Baga de secretis*, pp. 279–281.
[14] *R. v. Perrott*, 1 St. Tr. 1315–1531. See Black, pp. 472–474. *R. v. O'Cullon*, *Baga de secretis*, pp. 283–284.
[15] *Story's Case*, 1 St. Tr. 1087–1096.
[16] *Story's Case*, Dyer 300b pl. 38.
[17] *Story's Case*, Dyer 298 pl. 29.
[18] Dyer 360b pl. 6.

[19] *Baga de secretis*, pp. 259–261.
[20] *Baga de secretis*, pp. 263–264.
[21] *Baga de secretis*, p. 263.

Norfolk and his retainer Hickford showed that newer ideas were intertwined with older.[22] Both were accused of conspiring and imagining the deprivation of Elizabeth's crown and dignity and her death and destruction. Norfolk was also accused of compassing to incite sedition, to levy war and rebellion against the queen, "to change and alter the pure religion established in the kingdom," and to bring in foreign troops to wage a bitter war.[23] Significantly, the crown attorneys relied very heavily upon the concepts most directly derived from the statute of Edward III and tried to relate the other points to these major formulae. There was a sharp difference between the language of the indictment and the reasoning of the trial lawyers. It seemed that the legal mind balked at the creation of new constructive treasons. It also suggested the reticence of the crown to rely too heavily upon more recent statutory definitions. Thus, despite all the lofty rhetoric about depriving the queen of her royal dignity or crown imperial, the most useful concept still remained that of treachery expressed in levying war and in compasses and imaginings of her death. The trials of Hickford and Norfolk, therefore, pointed out clearly the confluence of religious, political, and international factors in the definition of high treason.

Subsequent cases produced a synthesis of these ideas under three major concepts: to destroy the queen, to subvert established religion, and to adhere to foreign powers. These ideas were operative in the earlier cases of the Jesuits, the earl of Arundel, Sir John Perrott, and Dr. Story. The union of the ideas of compassing Elizabeth's death and of subverting the established religion appeared in Somervyle's case (1583), Dr. Parry's case (1584/5), Shelley's and Babington's cases (1586), and in Dr. Lopez's case (1593/4).[24] No distinction was drawn between intending to kill the queen and intending to alter her established religion, a point also emphasized in the trials of Campion and the earl of Arundel. Together, these cases demonstrated that the concepts of treason which permeated the enacted law of the period had been integrated into the common law. New theoretical and practical views of treason had been also synthesized within the more traditional expressions of treason, so well illustrated in the trials of the earls of Essex and Southampton in 1601.[25] In a real sense, the case law had successfully related new ideas to the core idea of treachery which undergirded the idea of treason in 25 Edward III St. 5. c. 2.

While the foregoing cases might capture the more exciting aspects of treason, the last two groups of cases focused on less dramatic but equally significant ideas. The primary point of these cases was the relation of the subject to the law of the prince. For example, the justices decided in 6 Elizabeth Trinity term that judgment in treason for clipping the coin of England (under 5 Elizabeth c. 11), was none other than to be drawn and quartered.[26] Agan in 1570/1, the judges heard three cases involving either clipping or counterfeiting the coinage. Two of the three parties were sentenced to death while the third person received a pardon under the Great Seal.[27] In the case of John Conier, the justices had to determine the culpability of receivers of counterfeit money. While Conier was found guilty of receiving such false money and of aiding and comforting the counterfeiter, the bench refused to proceed to a judgment in treason upon the indictment.[28] While it was clear that Conier was an accessory and while it was a principle that in treasons all accessories were principals, the court refused to extend this concept to snare an accessory after the fact. It was a significant example of judicial restraint in that the opportunity to construct a new meaning of treason was not taken. It was a most narrow interpretation of the treason of counterfeiting that restricted the liability of accessories to before and during the acts of the principal.

Such attention to procedural safeguards was not unknown to the law of treason under Elizabeth. At times the ruling aided the crown, at times the subject. In either instance, the desire was to strike a balance between conflicting interests. Dyer, for example, reported that Saunders, Chief Baron and Whyddon, Justice held that if a man was arraigned for treason and held himself mute or would not answer directly to the crime, judgment was to be given as on one convicted.[29] This point was again sustained in the case of Dr. John Story.[30] Moreover, in the Duke of Norfolk's case, the judges ruled that in treason cases the accused was not allowed counsel and that the accused had to plead to the whole indictment either guilty or not guilty.[31] Only the jury, it was ruled in Hickford's trial, could find the accused not guilty of certain parts of an indictment.[32]

One of the more difficult questions was how to proceed against rebels who had fled the country; another was how to proceed against those who had been apprehended for treason. In the instance of those who had been captured and had confessed their crimes in the presence of three privy councillors, the judges ruled that such persons should not be indicted outside the county in which the offenses had occurred. Once indictments

---

[22] *Norfolk's Case*, 1 St. Tr. 957–1031; *Hickford's Case*, 1 St. Tr. 1042–1050.
[23] *Baga de secretis*, p. 268.
[24] *R. v. Somervyle*, *Baga de secretis*, pp. 272–273; *Parry's Case*, 1 St. Tr. 1095-1112; *Shelley's Case*, *Baga de secretis*, pp. 274–275; *Babington's Case*, *Baga de secretis*, pp. 276–278; *R. v. Lopez*, *Baga de secretis*, pp. 285–289. See also Black, pp. 376 377, 380–382, 408.
[25] 1 St. Tr. 1333–1360. See also Black, pp. 433, 439–441.

[26] *Wright's Case*, Dyer 296a pl. 21.
[27] *R. v. de Gawnt et al.*, *Baga de secretis*, pp. 265–267.
[28] *John Conier's Case*, Dyer 296a pl. 21.
[29] Dyer 205a pl. 4.
[30] Dyer 300b pl. 38.
[31] 1 St. Tr. 965–966.
[32] 1 St. Tr. 1044.

had been obtained in the appropriate county, it was then possible to remove the cases by writs of certiorari to the Queen's Bench or to special commissions of oyer and terminer in Middlesex. Individuals who pleaded not guilty were to be tried by jurors from the county in which the indictment was found, or by freeholders from the area and out of the county.[33] The second decision affected those who had fled the country, for the judges maintained that those who had fled could be indicted for treason and could be proceeded against for outlawry whether they had committed common law treasons or those defined by newer laws.[34] All these rulings tended to give the crown considerable advantage in prosecuting its cases despite the fact that crown lawyers did have to observe due process for the sake of the accused. It was also clear that these procedures were not viewed as mere technicalities but were viewed as integral to the obligations a prince owed to even the most disgusting subject. Moreover, it should be indicated that such safeguards tended to be derived from the case law rather than the enacted law, for in the latter instance, provisions were often ignored when concerned with the conduct of the trial. For example, Norfolk never had the opportunity actually to confront his accusers and examine them despite the frequent provisions of Elizabethan laws on that point.[35] Nevertheless, while rules were often bent for the advantage of the crown, the last report of the reign suggested that they could be bent for the subject. Indicted for treason, Linley was summoned to the bar in Easter term, 43 Elizabeth, whereupon he was asked why the court should not proceed upon the indictment. He then produced the queen's pardon without any writ of allowance for it. The clerk of the crown advised the court that the precedents allowed of the pardon without the writ of allowance in cases of treason but not of felony.[36] Justice had been tempered with mercy, a most singular event in Elizabethan treason cases.

3.

The most cogent statement of the Elizabethan judicial view of the nature of correct relations between prince and subject, the substance of the law of treason, came from Chief Justice Catlin in the Hickford case. To Hickford and others like him, Catlin stated that evil teachers and bad seedsmen had brought them to their sorry plight. Indeed, it was the greatest blot and infamy to be a traitor. He then put things in proper perspective:

It is the chiefest point of the duty of every natural and reasonable man, which by the gift of reason differeth from the beast, to know his prince and head, to be true to his head and prince. All the members are bound to obey the head; every man is bound to repair life, to lay out and expend goods, lands, and possessions, to forsake father, kindred, wife, children, and all.[37]

Subjects must first look to God, the prince of all princes, and then to the queen, their second prince and His deputy on earth. Bad seedsmen, the devil, and his ministers, had led into disloyalty like those who had stood before the justice. The disloyalty of the condemned turned the justice's thoughts to the nation's history. The country had suffered much from such perfidious acts. How foreigners constantly held up the histories of Henry II, Richard II, and Edward V "to the great infamy and slander of our country"![38] Surely such reminders of the past would have been enough to deter any conscientious subject. Yet, another example from the nation's past came to mind in the consideration of national and individual reputations, that concluded his oration:

As for them that seek fame by Treason, and by procuring the destruction of princes, where shall sound that fame? Shall the golden Trump of Fame and good Report, that Chaucer speaketh of? No; but the black Trump of Shame shall blow out their infamy for ever.[39]

The speech was indeed a fine rendering of the judicial understanding of the relations that bound prince and subject together. The idea of the prince as God's deputy on earth and head of the commonwealth hearkened back to the concept of *Liber Regalis* and the *Book of Homilies*. The God-given reason of the subject laid moral responsibilities upon him to function well as a member of an organic community regulated by divine and natural law in which the prince was a figure of Christ. History and literature confirmed from experience what men knew in their hearts to be true, that in the prince was individual and communal continuity and unity. The law of God and the law of man, then, were the bulwarks which protected the prince and commonwealth against the powers of evil expressed as mutability and chaos.

Understandably, the judicial contribution to the official doctrine of the prince might stress the mixed nature of the sovereign in the idea of the king's two bodies. The concept, contrary to Maitland's view, offered a suitable fiction to express the essence of political and social reality in Elizabethan England.[40] In this idea, physical and metaphysical threats to the integrity of prince and people could become articulated and could permit rational rebuttals. Even with this exalted status in the community, the prince did not emerge *legibus solutus*. Within legal thinking, he could not operate outside the laws and customs of the realm as defined and declared by the Prince in Parliament and expounded by the

---

[33] Dyer 286 pl. 44.
[34] Dyer 287a pl. 49.
[35] 1 St. Tr. 965–967.
[36] *Sir Henry Linley's Case*, Cro. Eliz. 814.
[37] 1 St. Tr. 1045.
[38] 1 St. Tr. 1046.
[39] 1 St. Tr. 1046.
[40] Frederic William Maitland, *Collected Papers* (Cambridge, 1911) 3: pp. 249f.

common law. Thus, it was clear that the ruler could not act unjustly for his actions were mediated through the law. Consequently, his subjects owed obedience to him through his laws and through their hearts and minds.[41]

While the law of treason emphasized the obligations an individual owed his prince because the latter never intended him harm, it also implied that these obligations legally defined by men were but a part of the law of nature and of God. On this point, jurists joined statesmen and churchmen. Together these three groups had indicated various implications of the fundamental assumption of responsibilities and obligations existing between ruler and ruled. However elaborated, this major concept of the official doctrine united prince and people in the service of God whose instruments they were and whose will they should reflect. As prince and people strove to glorify God on earth, He in turn would exalt them in heaven; this was the lesson so well expressed in the Wilton Diptych.

---

[41] Lacey B. Smith, "English Treason Trials and Confessions in the Sixteenth Century," *Jour. Hist. of Ideas* 15 (1954): pp. 471–498.

INDEX

Accession Day, the Elizabethan celebration of the, 7–8, 24–26
Allen, Cardinal William, 46

Babington, Gervase, 23
Bancroft, Richard, 27–28
Baumer, Franklin Le Van, 8
Book of Christian Prayers, A, 19
Book of Common Prayer, the, 7, 17–19, 27
Book of Homilies, the, 8, 17, 20, 29, 49

Catlin, Sir Robert, 49
Cecil, William Lord Burghley, and *The Execution of Justice in England* by, 8, 33–34, 36, 42
Chain of Being, the, 6, 7, 13, 15, 16
Chaucer, a judicial allusion to, 49
Church of England, the, Accession Day services of, 24–26; coronation rites of 10–16; Homily on Obedience used by, 20–21; occasional prayers and offices of, 18–19; Prayer Book services of, 17–19
Coronation Service, an analysis of the, 10, 11, 12–16
Corporation Sole, the, 8, 9, 49
Cosmic Dance, the, 6, 12, 15–16
Crown Imperial, the, 8, 44, 45
Cult of the Virgin Mary, the, and Elizabeth I, 6–8
Curteys, Richard, 21–22

Dickens, A. G., 6–7
Dunham, William Huse, Jr., 8–9, 44, 45

Edward of East Anglia, 5
Edward the Confessor, 5, 13, 17
Elizabeth I, the coronation of, 10–17; sermons preached before, 21–24; speeches of, to Parliament, 36–43; treasons against, 46–49; treason definitions in the reign of, 43–46
Etzioni, Amitai, 10

Geanakoplos, Deno J., 6–7
Guerard, Albert, 7
Great Seal, pardons under the, 48

Holdsworth, Sir William, 9
Homily on Obedience, the, 20–21

Indictments, in treason cases, 47–49

Jesuits, treason trials of, 44, 46, 48
Jewel, John, 22–23

Kantorowicz, Ernst, 6–8
King-in-Parliament, the idea of, 32, 36, 42
King's Peace, treason and the, 43
King's Two Bodies, the concept of the, 45, 47, 49

Laesa Majestas, the idea of, in the law, 43–44
Laudes Regiae, 7
Legg, J. Wickham, 7
Legibus Solutus, 49
Liber Regalis, 7, 11, 12–16, 49

Maitland, Frederic William, 9, 49
Mary Queen of Scots, 40, 47
Mary Tudor, 47
Middlesex, special commissions in, 49

Overton, William, 28

Oyer and Terminer, commissions of, 43, 49

Parliament, the High Court of, 31, 36, 42, 43
Persona Mixta, ecclesiastical ideas of the, 6–10, 15, 17
Popham, Sir John, 46
Primer of 1559, the, 19

Queen's Bench, the court of, 43, 49

Richard II, 5, 49
Roman Law, and the nature of treason, 45
Rudd, Anthony, 23–24

Sacerdotium and *Regnum,* the medieval concept of, 6–8
Sandys, Edwin, 23–29
Saunders, Sir Edward, 48
Shakespeare, *Richard II,* 5, 7
Smith, Lacey B., 9
Smith, Sir Thomas, *De Respublica Anglorum The Maner of Government of England,* 8, 30–33, 36, 42
Sorokim, Pitrim A., 9–10
Steward, Lord High, the court of the, 43
Strong, Roy C., 7

Treason, and the criminal law, 9, 43; the case law of, 46–49; statutes pertaining to, 43–46; trials for, and due process, 49

Whitgift, John, 22, 24–25
Wilson, Sir Thomas, *A Discourse Upon Usurye,* 8, 34–36, 42
Wilton Diptych, the, 5–7, 50

LIST OF CASES

R. v. Arundel, 46, 48
Babington's case, 48
R. v. Campion *et al.,* 46, 48
R. v. Chamberlain, 47
John Conier's case, 48
R. v. de Gavent *et al.,* 48
Duchy of Lancaster case, 9, 44
Earl of Essex case, 47, 48

John Felton's case, 46
R. v. Harleston, 47
Hickford's case, 48, 49
Sir Henry Linley's case, 49
Dr. Lopez's case, 48
Norfolk's case, 47, 48
R. v. O'Cullon, 47
Dr. Parry's case, 48

R. v. Perrott, 47, 48
R. v. Poole *et al.,* 47
Shelley's case, 48
Somervyle's case, 48
R. v. Southampton, 48
Story's case, 47, 48
R. v. Wentworth *et al.,* 47
Wright's case, 48

LIST OF STATUTES

25 Edward III, St. 5. c. 2, 9, 33, 43–45, 46, 47, 48
35 Henry VIII, c. 2, 47
1 Elizabeth c. 1, 44
1 Elizabeth c. 5, 45

5 Elizabeth c. 1, 44–46
5 Elizabeth c. 11, 48
13 Elizabeth c. 1, 45
13 Elizabeth c. 2, 44
14 Elizabeth c. 1, 45

14 Elizabeth c. 2, 46
18 Elizabeth c. 1, 45
23 Elizabeth c. 1, 44
27 Elizabeth c. 2, 44

TRANSACTIONS

OF THE

AMERICAN PHILOSOPHICAL SOCIETY

HELD AT PHILADELPHIA
FOR PROMOTING USEFUL KNOWLEDGE

NEW SERIES—VOLUME 66
1976

THE AMERICAN PHILOSOPHICAL SOCIETY
INDEPENDENCE SQUARE
PHILADELPHIA

1976

CONTENTS OF VOLUME 66

PART 1. The German Center Party, 1890–1906. JOHN K. ZEENDER.

PART 2. Perugia, 1260–1340: Conflict and Change in a Medieval Italian Urban Society SARAH RUBIN BLANSHEI.

PART 3. Crystals and Compounds: Molecular Structure and Composition in Nineteenth-century French Science. SEYMOUR H. MAUSKOPF.

PART 4. The Bourgeois Democrats of Weimar Germany. ROBERT A. POIS.

PART 5. The Persecution of Peter Olivi. DAVID BURR.

PART 6. Gaetano Filangieri and his *Science of Legislation*. MARCELLO MAESTRO.

PART 7. Recurrent Themes and Sequences in North American Indian-European Culture Contact. EDWARD McM. LARRABEE.

PART 8. Crown and Commonwealth: A Study in the Official Elizabethan Doctrine of the Prince. EDWARD O. SMITH.

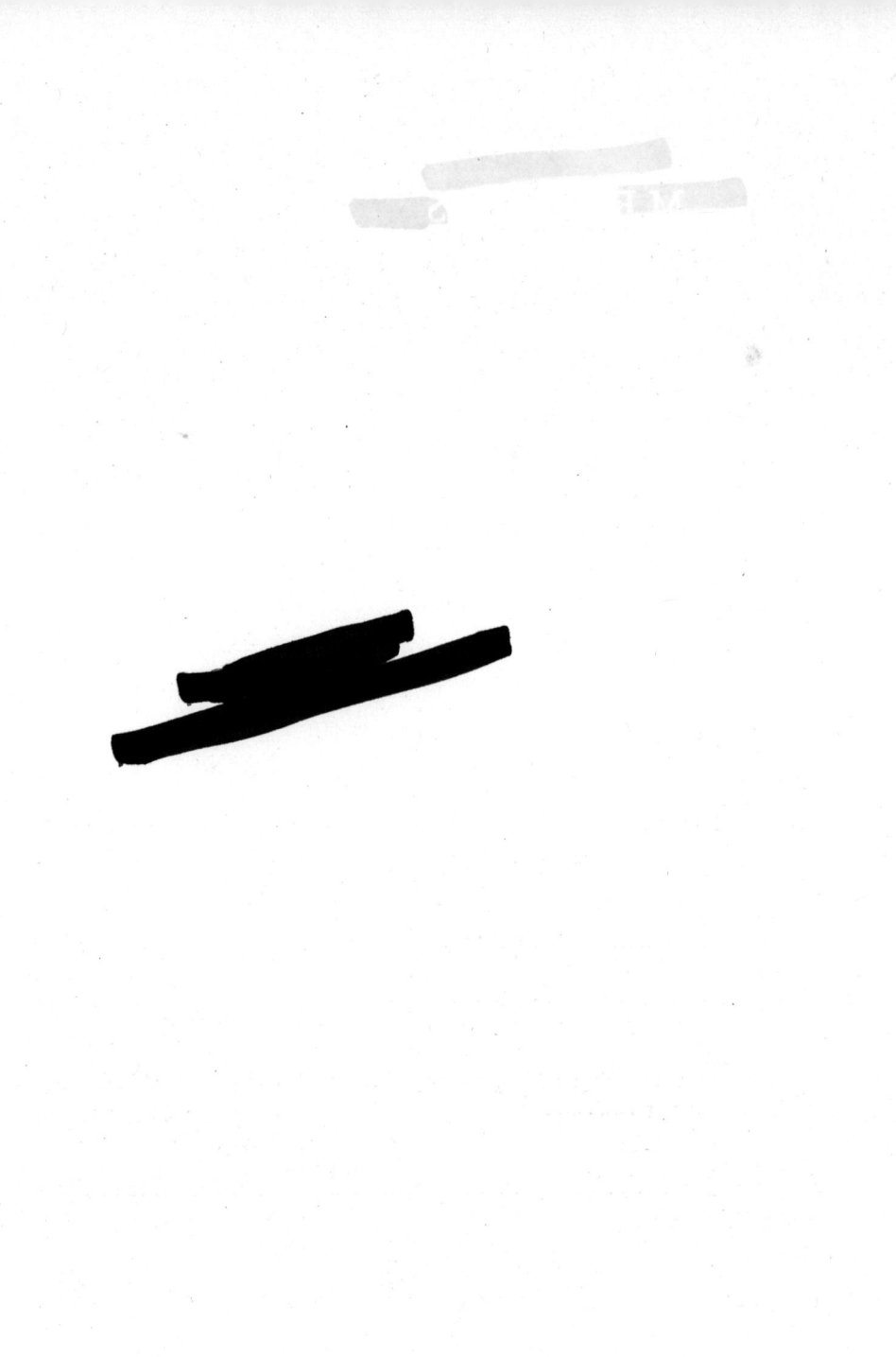

MEMOIRS

OF THE

AMERICAN PHILOSOPHICAL SOCIETY

Medical Men at the Siege of Boston, April, 1775–April, 1776: Problems of the Massachusetts and Continental Armies. PHILIP CASH.
Vol. 98. xiv, 185 pp., 11 figs., 1973. Paper. $3.00.

Crucial American Elections. ARTHUR S. LINK et al.
Vol. 99. x, 77 pp., 1973. $3.00.

John Beckley: Zealous Partisan in a Nation Divided. EDMUND BERKELEY and DOROTHY SMITH BERKELEY.
Vol. 100. xvi, 312 pp., 6 figs., 1973. $6.00.

Peter Tudebode: Historia de Hierosolymitano Itinere. JOHN HUGH HILL and LAURITA L. HILL.
Vol. 101. xii, 137 pp., 2 maps, 1974. $5.00.

Benjamin Franklin's Philadelphia Printing: A Descriptive Bibliography. C. WILLIAM MILLER.
Vol. 102. xc, 583 pp., illus., 1974. $40.00.

The Anschluss Movement in Austria and Germany, 1918–1919, and the Paris Peace Conference. ALFRED D. LOW.
Vol. 103. xiv, 495 pp., 4 figs., 4 maps, 1974. Paper. $8.00.

Studies in Pre-Vesalian Anatomy: Biography, Translations, Documents. L. R. LIND.
Vol. 104. xiv, 344 pp., 54 figs., 1975. $18.00.

A Kind of Power: The Shakespeare-Dickens Analogy. ALFRED B. HARBAGE. Jayne Lectures for 1974.
Vol. 105. x, 78 pp., 1975. $4.00.

A Venetian Family and Its Fortune, 1500–1900: The Donà and the Conservation of Their Wealth. JAMES C. DAVIS.
Vol. 106. xvi, 189 pp., 18 figs., 1975. $6.50.

Academica: Plato, Philip of Opus, and the Pseudo-Platonic Epinomis. LEONARDO TARÁN.
Vol. 107. viii, 417 pp., 1975. $20.00.

The Roman Catholic Church and the Creation of the Modern Irish State, 1878–1886. EMMET LARKIN.
Vol. 108. xiv, 412 pp., 2 figs., 1 map, 1975. Paper. $7.50.

Science and the Ante-Bellum American College. STANLEY M. GURALNICK.
Vol. 109. xiv, 227 pp., 1975. Paper. $5.00.

Hilary Abner Herbert: A Southerner Returns to the Union. HUGH B. HAMMETT.
Vol. 110. xvi, 264 pp., 20 figs., 1976. Paper. $5.00.

Census of the Exact Sciences in Sanskrit. Series A, Volume 3. DAVID PINGREE.
Vol. 111. vi, 208 pp., 1976. Paper. $15.00.

Cyriacus of Ancona's Journeys in the Propontis and the Northern Aegean, 1444–1445. EDWARD W. BODNAR and CHARLES MITCHELL.
Vol. 112. viii, 90 pp., 24 figs., 1976. Paper. $6.00.

The Autobiography of John Fitch. Edited by FRANK D. PRAGER.
Vol. 113. viii, 215 pp., 15 figs., 1976. Paper. $7.00.

TRANSACTIONS
OF THE
AMERICAN PHILOSOPHICAL SOCIETY

Gears from the Greeks: The Antikythera Mechanism—A Calendar Computer from *ca.* 80 B.C.   DEREK DE SOLLA PRICE.
Vol. 64, pt. 7, 70 pp., 45 figs., 1974. $5.00.

The Imperial Library in Southern Sung China, 1127–1279: A Study of the Organization and Operation of the Scholarly Agencies of the Central Government.   JOHN H. WINKELMAN.
Vol. 64, pt. 8, 61 pp., 8 figs., 1974. $5.00.

The Czechoslovak Heresy and Schism: The Emergence of a National Czechoslovak Church.   LUDVIK NEMEC.
Vol. 65, pt. 1, 78 pp., 1975. $6.00.

Distractions of Peace During War: The Lloyd George Government's Reactions to Woodrow Wilson, December, 1916–November, 1918.   STERLING J KERNEK.
Vol. 65, pt. 2, 117 pp., 1975. $6.00.

Classification and Development of North American Indian Cultures: A Statistical Analysis of the Driver-Massey Sample.   HAROLD E. DRIVER and JAMES L. COFFIN.
Vol. 65, pt. 3, 120 pp., 12 figs., 5 maps, 1975. $7.00.

The Flight of Birds.   CRAWFORD H. GREENEWALT.
Vol. 65, pt. 4, 67 pp., 41 figs., 1 pl., 1975. $7.00.

A Guide to Francis Galton's English Men of Science.   VICTOR L. HILTS.
Vol. 65, pt. 5, 85 pp., 6 figs., 1975. $5.00.

Justice in Medieval Russia: Muscovite Judgment Charters (*Pravye Gramoty*) of the Fifteenth and Sixteenth Centuries.   ANN M. KLEIMOLA.
Vol. 65, pt. 6, 93 pp., 1975. $5.00.

The Sculpture of Taras.   JOSEPH COLEMAN CARTER.
Vol. 65, pt. 7, 196 pp., 72 pls., 2 maps, 1975. $18.00.

The Franciscans in South Germany, 1400–1530: Reform and Revolution.   PAUL L. NYHUS.
Vol. 65, pt. 8, 47 pp., 1975. $3.00.

The German Center Party, 1890–1906.   JOHN K. ZEENDER.
Vol. 66, pt. 1, 125 pp., 2 figs., 1976. $7.50.

Perugia, 1260–1340: Conflict and Change in a Medieval Italian Urban Society.   SARAH RUBIN BLANSHEI.
Vol. 66, pt. 2, 128 pp., 2 maps, 1976. $8.50.

Crystals and Compounds: Molecular Structure and Composition in Nineteenth-century French Science.   SEYMOUR H. MAUSKOPF.
Vol. 66, pt. 3, 82 pp., 4 figs., 1976. $4.50.

The Bourgeois Democrats of Weimar Germany.   ROBERT A. POIS
Vol. 66, pt. 4, 117 pp., 1976. $6.00.

The Persecution of Peter Olivi.   DAVID BURR.
Vol. 66, pt. 5, 98 pp., 1976. $6.00

Gaetano Filangieri and His *Science of Legislation*.   MARCELLO MAESTRO.
Vol. 66, pt. 6, 76 pp., 4 figs. 1976. $6.00.

Recurrent Themes and Sequences in North American Indian-European Culture Contact.   EDWARD MCM. LARRABEE.
Vol. 66, pt. 7, 52 pp., 6 figs., 3 maps, 1976. $6.00.